RSYA

D0990734

JAN   2007

The Birmingham Church Bombings

by Stephen Currie

LUCENT BOOKS

An imprint of Thomson Gale, a part of The Thomson Corporation

THOMSON
™
GALE

Detroit • New York • San Francisco • San Diego • New Haven, Conn. • Waterville, Maine • London • Munich

© 2006 Thomson Gale, a part of The Thomson Corporation.

Thomson and Star Logo are trademarks and Gale and Lucent Books are registered trademarks used herein under license.

For more information, contact
Lucent Books
27500 Drake Rd.
Farmington Hills, MI 48331-3535
Or you can visit our Internet site at http://www.gale.com

ALL RIGHTS RESERVED.
No part of this work covered by the copyright hereon may be reproduced or used in any form or by any means—graphic, electronic, or mechanical, including photocopying, recording, taping, Web distribution, or information storage retrieval systems—without the written permission of the publisher.

Every effort has been made to trace the owners of copyrighted material.

LIBRARY OF CONGRESS CATALOGING-IN-PUBLICATION DATA

Currie, Stephen, 1960–
  The Birmingham church bombings / by Stephen Currie.
    p. cm. — (Crime scene investigations)
  Includes bibliographical references and index.
  ISBN 1-59018-842-X (hard cover : alk. paper) 1. Bombing investigation—Alabama—Birmingham. 2. Bombings—Alabama—Birmingham. 3. African Americans—Crimes against—Alabama—Birmingham. 4. Trials (Murder)—Alabama—Birmingham. 5. Hate crimes—Alabama—Birmingham. I. Title. II. Series: Crime scene investigations series.
  HV8079.B62C87 2006
  364.152'309761781—dc22

                                                            2005037625

Printed in the United States of America

Crime Scene

Y 364.1523 C936b 2006
Currie, Stephen, 1960-
The Birmingham church bombing

Contents

Foreword

The popularity of crime scene and investigative crime shows on television has come as a surprise to many who work in the field. The main surprise is the concept that crime scene analysts are the true crime solvers, when in truth, it takes dozens of people, doing many different jobs, to solve a crime. Often, the crime scene analyst's contribution is a small one. One Minnesota forensic scientist says that the public "has gotten the wrong idea. Because I work in a lab similar to the ones on *CSI*, people seem to think I'm solving crimes left and right— just me and my microscope. They don't believe me when I tell them that it's the investigators that are solving crimes, not me."

Crime scene analysts do have an important role to play, however. Science has rapidly added a whole new dimension to gathering and assessing evidence. Modern crime labs can match a hair of a murder suspect to one found on a murder victim, for example, or recover a latent fingerprint from a threatening letter, or use a powerful microscope to match tool marks made during the wiring of an explosive device to a tool in a suspect's possession.

Probably the most exciting of the forensic scientist's tools is DNA analysis. DNA can be found in just one drop of blood, a dribble of saliva on a toothbrush, or even the residue from a fingerprint. Some DNA analysis techniques enable scientists to tell with certainty, for example, whether a drop of blood on a suspect's shirt is that of a murder victim.

While these exciting techniques are now an essential part of many investigations, they cannot solve crimes alone. "DNA doesn't come with a name and address on it," says the Minnesota forensic scientist. "It's great if you have someone in custody to match the sample to, but otherwise, it doesn't help. That's the investigator's job. We can have all the great DNA evidence in the world, and without a suspect, it will just sit on the shelf. We've all seen cases with very little forensic evidence get solved by the resourcefulness of a detective."

While forensic specialists get the most media attention today, the work of detectives still forms the core of most criminal investigations. Their job, in many ways, has changed little over the years. Most cases are still solved through the persistence and determination of a criminal detective whose work may be anything but glamorous. Many cases require routine, even mind-numbing tasks. After the July 2005 bombings in London, for example, police officers sat in front of video players watching thousands of hours of closed-circuit television tape from security cameras throughout the city, and as a result were able to get the first images of the bombers.

The Lucent Books Crime Scene Investigations series explores the variety of ways crimes are solved. Titles cover particular crimes such as murder, specific cases such as the killing of three civil rights workers in Mississippi, or the role specialists such as medical examiners play in solving crimes. Each title in the series demonstrates the ways a crime may be solved, from the various applications of forensic science and technology to the reasoning of investigators. Sidebars examine both the limits and possibilities of the new technologies and present crime statistics, career information, and step-by-step explanations of scientific and legal processes.

The Crime Scene Investigations series strives to be both informative and realistic about how members of law enforcement— criminal investigators, forensic scientists, and others—solve crimes, for it is essential that student researchers understand that crime solving is rarely quick or easy. Many factors—from a detective's dogged pursuit of one tenuous lead to a suspect's careless mistakes to sheer luck to complex calculations computed in the lab—are all part of crime solving today.

A Troubled City

To African Americans in Birmingham, Alabama, during the early 1960s, the Sixteenth Street Baptist Church was a busy and vital place. The graceful church building near Birmingham's downtown district housed an all-black congregation that was among the city's largest and most influential. In addition to holding well-attended Sunday morning services and offering Christian education classes for both children and adults, the church also aided the poor and needy in Birmingham's black community. Members took justifiable pride in their church and the role it played in making Birmingham a better place for African Americans.

But beyond the walls of the church, Birmingham during these years was a troubled city. Since the late 1950s, the city had been at the forefront of the civil rights movement—a political and social struggle meant to improve the lives of the African Americans of the South. Through nonviolent protests, demonstrations, and marches, some of them led by nationally known figures such as Martin Luther King Jr., the African Americans of Birmingham had been agitating for economic and political equality and an end to racial injustice. They pushed white leaders to create a fairer and more inclusive city that would provide greater opportunities for all.

Birmingham's African Americans certainly had legitimate complaints. For one, the city followed a policy of segregation, or strict separation of the races. By law, for example, blacks could not attend the same schools as whites. Neither could they sit in the same sections of movie theaters, eat in the same restaurants, or use the same public restrooms. Though segregation

Civil rights leader Martin
Luther King Jr., speaks at a
1963 news conference in
Birmingham, Alabama.

prevailed throughout the South, it was particularly notable in Birmingham, which King called "the most segregated city in America."[1]

Nor was enforced separation of the races the only issue faced by Birmingham's black community. African Americans suffered both politically and economically. Though in theory blacks in Birmingham had the right to vote, the reality was that they encountered huge obstacles if they tried to do so. Most African Americans held low-paying, menial jobs with little possibility for advancement, and many types of employment were closed to black people. The city had no black firefighters, for instance, and the white business leaders who owned downtown stores refused to hire black clerks. The average salary of Birmingham's African Americans, as a result, was far below that of the average white resident of the city.

Most of Alabama's whites were satisfied with these circumstances and enthusiastically defended segregation. The tone was set by Alabama's governor, George Wallace, first elected in 1962. "Segregation now . . . segregation tomorrow . . . segregation forever,"[2] Wallace thundered during his inauguration speech; his words were cheered by many of Birmingham's white citizens. Maintaining segregation in Alabama's public schools was Wallace's particular concern. During the early 1960s, when a series of federal laws and judges' rulings required the state's school systems to desegregate, Wallace pledged to disobey the government. Several times, he made a show of standing at the entrances of all-white schools in order to block African American children from attending.

Violence and Terror

Birmingham's city officials were also vehement supporters of segregation. When the federal government ordered the city to end segregation in its whites-only public schools, Birmingham city commissioner Eugene "Bull" Connor pledged to shut down every school rather than submit to the ruling. Though in the end Connor did not carry through his threat, his readiness to

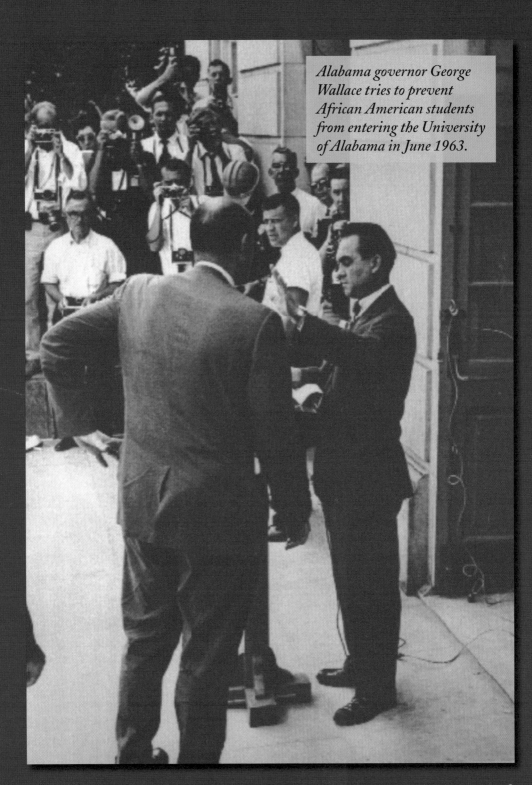

Alabama governor George Wallace tries to prevent African American students from entering the University of Alabama in June 1963.

Birmingham police routinely used attack dogs to quell demonstrations, a tactic that came to light in 1963 with the publication of this photo of a police dog attacking a protester.

defy the law won widespread support from the city's white citizens. And municipal leaders did close the entire city park system rather than obey a federal judge's order to open park facilities to the black community.

More ominously, members of Birmingham's white population also used violence to frighten and intimidate blacks. That was particularly true where civil rights protests were concerned. Most civil rights leaders preached a policy of nonviolence, urging protesters to remain peaceful. For the most part, the blacks who took part in these demonstrations were careful not to provoke white onlookers. Yet angry white crowds often responded with fury. "Some people . . . would throw rocks and cans and different things at us,"[3] a Birmingham protester recalled.

City officials used violence to control and harass protesters as well. During the spring of 1963, for instance, Bull

Connor ordered police officers to use attack dogs and fire hoses to disperse activists. Both caused injuries. The dogs were trained to bite on command; the hoses, as one writer noted, were "capable of tearing bark from a tree at one hundred yards."[4] Americans across the country read descriptions of protesters pinned against walls by water shooting from the hoses, and a widely circulated photograph of the time showed a terrified protester being attacked by a police dog.

Bombs and Explosions

Worse still, a few ardent segregationists used bombs to frighten and harass the city's African Americans. In August 1963, for instance, bombs exploded at the homes of two of Birmingham's most prominent black citizens. And in 1962, late-night explosions badly damaged several black churches throughout the city, all of them smaller and less well known than Sixteenth Street Baptist. These explosions caused enormous property damage, but as of September 1963 had resulted in no serious injuries or deaths. Nonetheless, African Americans throughout Birmingham were well aware that another, even more damaging attack could follow at any time. The question was not so much whether there would be such an attack, but when it would come, and where.

The attack did indeed come—and is still remembered today as one of the most notorious crimes of the civil rights era. Unfortunately, despite the violence of the bombing and the widespread publicity regarding the case, the crime proved exceptionally difficult to solve. In the end, nearly four decades passed before the perpetrators were brought to justice. Investigators had to deal with obstacles ranging from an almost complete lack of physical evidence and a series of possibly unreliable eyewitnesses to government secrecy and the cultural climate of 1960s Alabama. Still, investigators never entirely stopped trying to solve the crime. As a result of their perseverance, justice was only delayed in the Birmingham civil rights case. It was not denied.

CHAPTER 1

The Crime

Despite the ever-present threat of violence, the morning of September 15, 1963, began little differently from any other Sunday at the Sixteenth Street Baptist Church. By 9:30 that morning, well before the main service was to begin, the church was already bustling with activity. As on any other Sunday morning, some members of the congregation were engaged in Christian education classes. Others made a point of arriving early to have time to socialize with friends and acquaintances. And still others were already at work preparing for the upcoming service.

The main service that September 15 had a special theme. In an effort to draw the church's children and teenagers more deeply into the life of the congregation, pastor John Cross had declared the service a Youth Day celebration. Cross had enlisted the church's young people to serve as ushers, provide music, and play various other roles during the morning worship service. Eager to look their best, several of the girls scheduled to participate had taken great pains fixing their hair and picking out their clothes before leaving for church. Several members of the congregation noticed their efforts. "My, don't you look pretty,"[5] one woman said as eleven-year-old Denise McNair arrived at church.

Such compliments notwithstanding, five girls gathered in the women's restroom on the lowest level of the church at about 10:15 to make final adjustments to their clothing and hair. The girls were Denise McNair, twelve-year-old Sarah Collins, and fourteen-year-olds Cynthia Wesley, Carole Robertson, and Addie Mae Collins; Addie Mae was Sarah Collins's sister. The girls straightened their clothes, retied the

Police and emergency workers survey the damage to the Sixteenth Street Baptist Church on September 15, 1963.

sashes on their dresses, and washed their hands one last time. "They were excited," wrote one commentator. "They were nervous. They were happy."[6] It was almost time for the Youth Day service.

But the service never took place. At 10:22 that morning, the people in the church heard a noise that some described as a thunderclap, others as a dull thud. A streak of fire leaped toward the ceiling. The air was filled with the odor of burning. Metal chairs slammed into walls; wooden benches were reduced to splinters. Flying debris and violent gusts shattered the face of Jesus in a stained glass window. "We've been bombed!"[7] cried a worshipper. The violence that had plagued other Birmingham black churches had come to Sixteenth Street Baptist.

Tragedy

In spite of the massive damage that the explosion inflicted on the church building, most worshippers were able to reach an outside door under their own power. A few were bleeding, but none appeared to have suffered life-threatening injuries. Surveying the dozens of people standing on the sidewalk, Cross was cautiously optimistic that all the members of his congregation had survived the blast. When Cross ventured back inside to perform a cursory check of the building, he found no one caught beneath the wreckage. Briefly, his spirits rose. "Good," he told himself. "I don't see a single person trapped."[8]

But the pastor's optimism was premature. Though most of the church had been damaged, one section along the building's northeastern wall had been almost completely destroyed. Parishioners quickly realized that the explosion had centered on this wall. The blast had vaporized an outside staircase and blown a hole 50 feet

By the Numbers

48

Unsolved race-based bombings in Birmingham between 1948 and 1957

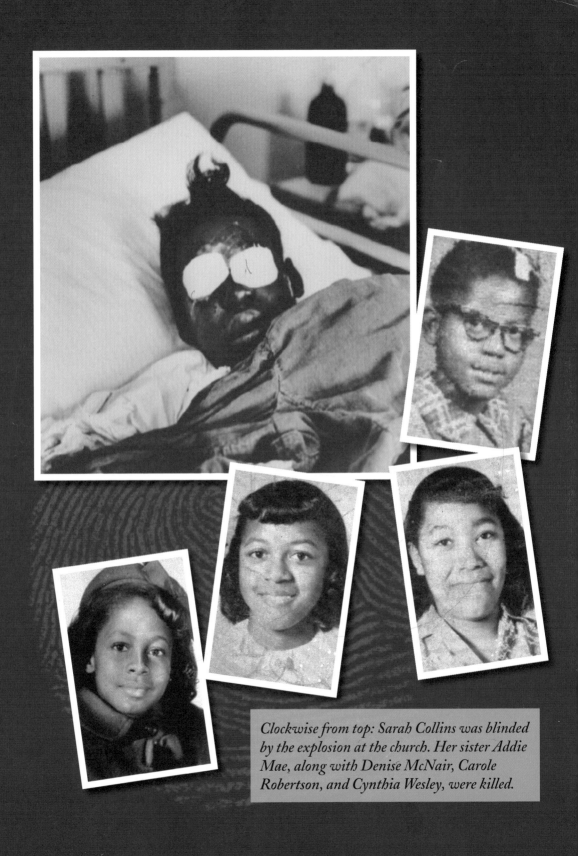

Clockwise from top: Sarah Collins was blinded by the explosion at the church. Her sister Addie Mae, along with Denise McNair, Carole Robertson, and Cynthia Wesley, were killed.

(15m) square in the exterior wall. On the other side of the hole, worshippers realized, was the lowest level of the church—specifically, the women's restroom.

As a crowd gathered on the sidewalk, worshippers remembered that several girls had gone into the restroom just a few minutes before the explosion. Alarmed, some of the church members began digging into the debris. They were soon joined by civil defense workers who arrived on the scene. Before long, the diggers were appalled to find the bodies of Carole Robertson, Denise McNair, Cynthia Wesley, and Addie Mae Collins. All four girls, it was clear, had been killed instantly by the force of the blast. Of the five people in the restroom at 10:22 that morning, only Sarah Collins had survived—and she would spend the next two months hospitalized with severe injuries.

A funeral service for three of the four young bombing victims held on September 18, 1963, drew a large crowd.

Reaction

The bombing of the Sixteenth Street Baptist Church almost instantly became big news across America. Even before the explosion, most Americans were aware that a bitter civil rights struggle was taking place in Birmingham. The speeches of Martin Luther King and the belligerent words of Governor George Wallace had been featured in the news media across the nation. So had photos of the attack dogs and fire hoses used against protesters by Birmingham police. The determined opposition to school desegregation, the closing of the park system, the frequent marches for the rights of African Americans—all were familiar to people across the country, whether they had a connection with Birmingham or not.

The blast at Sixteenth Street Baptist, however, was different. Now, the violence in Birmingham had caused deaths—and worse, the deaths of four innocent children. Americans throughout the nation struggled to understand how that could have happened. For many, it seemed inconceivable that anyone could have deliberately caused such an explosion. Except among the most virulent of racists, the result was deep sorrow for the victims of the blast and deep anger toward whoever had planted the bomb. More than the previous year's bombings of Birmingham churches, more even than the use of powerful hoses and police dogs, the September 15 blast angered and appalled those who heard the news.

Chicago native and civil rights advocate Diane Nash was just one of many who cried upon hearing that this bombing, unlike earlier explosions at Birmingham churches, had taken the lives of four young girls. Like other African Americans across the nation, Nash and her husband felt a personal connection with the girls who died in the blast. As Nash recalled years afterward, "We felt like our own children had been killed."[9]

That feeling was most obviously shared by Birmingham's African Americans. A few days after the bombing, two thousand mourners—most of them black and many unacquainted

with the girls and their families—crowded into a nearby church to attend a joint funeral service for Addie Mae Collins, Cynthia Wesley, and Denise McNair. (Carole Robertson's parents chose to have her buried in a separate service.) About five thousand more gathered outside the building. Many of the mourners were in tears. Others were furious. Most were both. "You know how I feel?" raged Denise McNair's grandfather. "I feel like blowing the whole town up!"[10]

Birmingham lawyer Chuck Morgan decried the violent act committed against the girls.

"A Terrible Event"

The feelings of sorrow and outrage were by no means confined to blacks. Many whites who lived outside the South, in particular, experienced similar emotions. Burke Marshall, a government official originally from New Jersey, recalled the bombing as "a terrible event because of its cruelty, its futility, [and its] senselessness."[11] Donations and offers of support poured into Birmingham from communities hundreds or even thousands of miles from Alabama. One city council in Michigan collected a thousand dollars to distribute among the families of the murdered girls. In California, Los Angeles County canceled government meetings in memory of the girls who had died.

Those southern whites who supported the civil rights movement were angry as well. Birmingham lawyer Chuck Morgan, for instance, was deeply shaken when he heard the news of the bombing. In a speech given to a local business organization and later reworked for publication in the national press, Morgan mourned the four girls and attacked the community that had produced such violence. To Morgan, the bombing seemed like a repudiation of all the work he and other white southern moderates had done to build a more equitable society. "Birmingham is not a dying city," he told his listeners. "It is dead."[12]

Even some ardent racists expressed revulsion at the deaths of the four young churchgoers. A white couple in a car plastered with Confederate flags—a common symbol of support for segregation at the time—stopped by Denise McNair's home to offer their condolences to her father. Newspapers in Birmingham and elsewhere in the South published editorials condemning the bombing. Birmingham's all-white city council sent telegrams of support and sorrow to the families of the murdered girls. Even Alabama's segregationist governor, George Wallace, described the bombing as a "dastardly act by a demented fool."[13]

The Ku Klux Klan

But Wallace and the Birmingham city council did not speak for all white supremacists. Privately, some staunch segregationists in the South cheered the bombing and the destruction it had created. These whites were enraged by the civil rights movement and its challenge to the racial divide in the South, and they were delighted that someone had struck back. In their opinion,

Two More Victims

The four girls killed in the blast at the Sixteenth Street Baptist Church were not the only victims of racial violence in Birmingham on September 15, 1963. Later that day, there was a rock-throwing incident that involved black teenagers; accounts differ as to whether they were engaged in a fight with white teenagers or throwing rocks at passing white drivers. In either case, when police appeared on the scene, a sixteen-year-old Birmingham resident named Johnny Robinson tried to run away. Police shot him in the back, killing him.

That same afternoon, a thirteen-year-old African American boy named Virgil Ware was riding on the handlebars of a bicycle pedaled by his brother James. Two white youths, who had apparently come from a prosegregation rally, drove up on a motor scooter and fired at the Ware brothers. "Virgil fell," reported James Ware, "and I said, get up Virgil, and he said, I can't, I'm shot." Virgil Ware died soon afterward.

Quoted in *Time* "The Sunday School Bombing," September 27, 1963, no page number available.

By the Numbers

21

Pieces of glass embedded in Sarah Collins's face by the explosion

the worshippers at the Sixteenth Street church had gotten what they deserved.

This attitude was especially common among the members of a white supremacist group known as the Ku Klux Klan. Since its founding after the Civil War, the Klan, as it was often called, had a history of brutalizing and terrorizing blacks who tried to assert their rights. A powerful force in national politics throughout the 1920s, the Klan had become relatively inactive during the next few decades, but with the coming of the civil rights movement in the late 1950s, it had been reborn. By 1963, it had once more become a vigorous organization across much of the South.

The Klansmen of the 1920s had come from all social classes of white society. In the 1960s, though, Klan members were overwhelmingly blue-collar, poorly educated, and unskilled. They tended also to be impulsive, violent, and angry. Historian Diane McWhorter described one Birmingham Klan member, Bobby Frank Cherry, as a "trucker with an eighth-grade education, no upper front teeth, a 'Bobby' tattoo on his arm, seven kids, and a wife he beat and cheated on."[14] Similar descriptions applied to many of Cherry's fellow Klan members.

Secrecy characterized the Klan during the 1960s. As part of their initiation into the group, members had to swear not to discuss Klan rituals and activities with anyone outside the organization. The penalty for breaking this code of silence could be death. Since the Klan was often involved in illegal acts, anonymity was essential. Most of the Klan's meetings and other activities were carried out at night. If members thought they might be seen and recognized by the general public, they wore long white robes and hoods that covered their faces.

The secrecy of the Klan helped build cohesiveness among its members. As individuals, Klansmen struggled to hold jobs and to make ends meet. But as members of the Ku Klux Klan, they were a force to be feared. The rituals of the organization, the mystery of its membership rolls, the insistence on secrecy—all unified the members and allowed them to band together against a common enemy: African Americans, the only people in the South who were widely viewed as beneath them. As one later commentator put it, the Klan gave these white men "a sense of place and power in a world that often afforded them neither."[15]

The Klan and the FBI

Despite the Ku Klux Klan's emphasis on secrecy, law enforcement officials usually knew in what parts of the country the Klan was active and how much of a threat the organization presented in any given place. Because of the bitterness of the civil rights struggle in Birmingham, Klan activity in and around

The Ku Klux Klan, members of which are seen here at a 1966 cross burning, applauded the church bombing.

the city was particularly high—and potentially deadly. Over the previous few years, in fact, the national government had instructed its chief law enforcement agency, the Federal Bureau of Investigation (FBI), to monitor the activities of Birmingham's Klansmen. In particular, federal officials hoped to find evidence that the local klaverns, or Klan chapters, had been involved in earlier bombings of Birmingham's black churches.

The FBI had hundreds of cases nationwide and could not spare many of its resources to tracking the Klan members of Birmingham. Still, the agents charged with this task had made some progress. Much of what they learned had come to them through a local Klan member named Gary Thomas Rowe. Though Rowe had been recruited by a local klavern, he did not

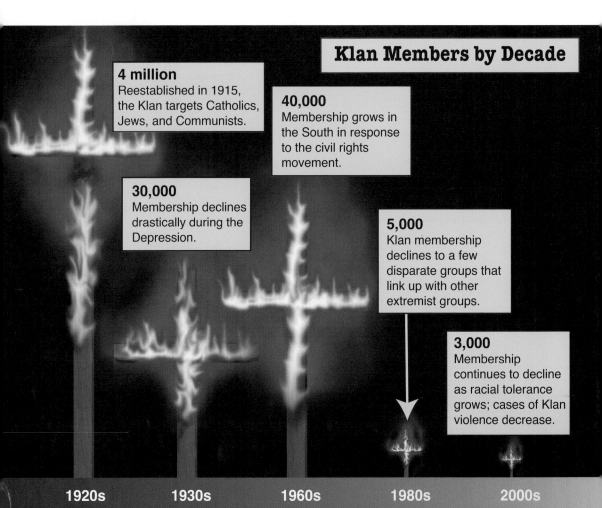

Klan Members by Decade

4 million
Reestablished in 1915, the Klan targets Catholics, Jews, and Communists.

40,000
Membership grows in the South in response to the civil rights movement.

30,000
Membership declines drastically during the Depression.

5,000
Klan membership declines to a few disparate groups that link up with other extremist groups.

3,000
Membership continues to decline as racial tolerance grows; cases of Klan violence decrease.

1920s   1930s   1960s   1980s   2000s

truly support the goals of the organization. Indeed, unknown to his fellow Klansmen, he was actually passing on information about the group to the FBI. After each meeting of his klavern, Rowe secretly met with federal officials and told them what had happened that night. The FBI agents, in turn, paid him for the information he supplied.

With Rowe's assistance, federal agents had been able to identify many, if not most, local Klansmen. However, Rowe's reports were not particularly useful in preventing further violence or arresting those who had carried out illegal activity in the past. In fact, Rowe told FBI agents, the men of his klavern spent most of their time talking, not doing. "I thought we was going to . . . [learn] how to throw bricks . . . burn the buildings, flog the people," he explained. "But we didn't. It was like 'so and so' was sick this week, we're going to take up a little collection."[16]

FBI informer Gary Thomas Rowe was able to infiltrate the Birmingham Ku Klux Klan.

Still, Rowe's reports left no doubt that Birmingham's Klansmen did stop talking long enough to carry out at least some violent acts. Rowe made it clear that Klan members had frequently beaten black protesters during the early 1960s. And though federal agents had been unable to prove Klan participation in the earlier church bombings, the FBI continued to believe that local klaverns were responsible. Thus, when the bomb went off at the Sixteenth Street Baptist Church that September morning in 1963, the members of Birmingham's Klan chapters were among the initial suspects.

The Birmingham Police

The bombing had taken place within Birmingham, so technically the case was the responsibility of the city's police department. The first law enforcement agents on the scene were

Police officers with leashed German shepherds keep a close eye on a protest rally at a Birmingham park in 1963.

members of Birmingham's police force, supplemented by state highway patrol officers. But many black Birmingham residents were not willing to leave the investigation solely in the hands of the local police. Some feared that Birmingham's police force lacked the resources necessary to take on a case of this magnitude. More seriously, though, some questioned whether the city police force would really do its best to solve the crime.

This distrust was warranted. The Birmingham police had shown little interest in investigating violence against civil rights protesters. The department had not yet solved the earlier bombings of churches and homes of prominent African Americans and did not seem to consider the cases to be high priorities. For that matter, the police had not hesitated to use violence against the city's African Americans who took part in the civil rights movement. Black Birmingham residents had not forgotten the dogs and the powerful hoses used by local police to disrupt peaceful protests just months earlier.

There were persistent rumors, too, that some members of Birmingham's law enforcement community were actually members of the Ku Klux Klan—or at the very least looked the other way while Klansmen carried out their violence against blacks. "The police didn't care," recalled Tom Cherry, one of the seven children of Klan member Bobby Frank Cherry. "You could do just about whatever you wanted to a black person and not get in trouble [in Birmingham]."[17] Under the circumstances, the city's African Americans and their supporters feared that the local police would not work hard to find those responsible for the bombing.

For that matter, few civil rights activists trusted state and local officials at any level. African Americans knew that virtually every important politician in Alabama was a segregationist. Even though Governor Wallace had condemned the church bombing, no civil rights leaders expected him to order an exhaustive investigation into the crime. In fact, many believed that Wallace and his political allies were indirectly responsible for the disaster. By defying federal attempts to bring integration to Alabama, these activists charged, Wallace had made it acceptable for fringe elements such as the Ku Klux Klan to intimidate and kill African Americans. "The blood of our little children is on your hands,"[18] Martin Luther King told Wallace.

King's view was echoed—and extended—by Chuck Morgan, the white Birmingham lawyer who favored civil rights. In his speech to business leaders, Morgan blamed the explosion not just on the unknown bomber, nor on Wallace and his friends, but on all Alabamians who supported the governor and his racist policies. "Every person in this community who has in any way contributed to the popularity of hatred," Morgan charged, "is at least as guilty, or more so, as the demented fool who threw that bomb."[19]

Kennedy and Hoover

Given their concerns about city and state police forces, civil rights leaders called for the national government to hand the

President John Kennedy gives an address to the American people regarding the civil rights crisis in Alabama in the summer of 1963.

Hoover and the Kennedys

The FBI was the investigative arm of the federal Department of Justice. In theory at least, J. Edgar Hoover reported to the head of this department, U.S. attorney general Robert Kennedy, who in addition to being a member of President John Kennedy's administration was also the president's brother. Civil rights leaders saw Robert Kennedy as a strong ally, and while many were less certain of John Kennedy's enthusiasm for

Robert Kennedy (right) speaks with FBI director J. Edgar Hoover in 1963.

their cause, most found the president generally supportive of civil rights. With both Kennedys outranking Hoover, the investigation should have been under the control of the Kennedy brothers.

But over his many years as director of the FBI, Hoover had developed a secretive leadership style and a great deal of power. By 1963, he ran the FBI more or less as he chose, paying little attention even to direct orders from his bosses and refusing to share information with anyone. The Kennedy brothers did not challenge Hoover's leadership style or authority. The result was that the federal investigation of the church bombing was actually controlled by Hoover with little input from his superiors.

investigation over to the FBI. The bureau had occasionally been summoned to work on civil rights cases in the past; a 1960 law explicitly gave it the authority to become involved in these cases even if local and state authorities objected. As a large federal agency under national control, moreover, the FBI would not be subject to the influence of Wallace and his supporters. Civil rights leaders were pleased when President John Kennedy announced that he would make the FBI the lead investigative agency in the hunt for the church bombers.

Nonetheless, few African Americans in Birmingham were enthusiastic supporters of the bureau. Even after the 1960 law allowing FBI participation in civil rights investigations, FBI director J. Edgar Hoover had been reluctant to order his agents to work on these cases. Hoover complained that civil rights leaders expected too much of his department. He argued that state and local officials should take charge of cases that concerned civil rights. In addition, Hoover had taken an intense personal dislike to King and several other movement leaders.

Still, no civil rights leader could fault Hoover's immediate response to Kennedy's order. Within hours of the bombing, dozens of interrogators, administrators, and technical experts associated with the bureau began pouring into Birmingham. Other FBI agents followed potential leads in various southern cities; still others worked on the case from bureau headquarters in Washington, D.C.

According to Hoover, the FBI devoted more agents to this case than it had to any single event since 1934, nearly thirty years earlier, when the department had launched a furious national hunt for a notorious criminal named John Dillinger. Even if that claim was exaggerated—and some believed it was—no one could doubt that Hoover was putting enormous resources into the church bombing case. The investigation seemed to be off to a promising start.

The Investigation Begins

The investigators who converged on Birmingham after the bombing of the Sixteenth Street Baptist Church used a variety of techniques to deduce who had planted the bomb. One of their highest priorities was to undertake a thorough study of the crime scene. The investigators charged with this task—members of the Birmingham police department as well as the FBI—knew that they might not find useful evidence among the ruins of the church. The intensity of the explosion, after all, had leveled much of the area near where the bomb had been placed. However, if a fragment of dynamite, a partial fingerprint, or even a shoelace had somehow survived the blast, such evidence could help to solve the case.

The first task was to determine what type of explosive had caused the blast. This part of the investigation proved easy. The noise made by the blast was consistent with the noise made by dynamite explosions, and the odor in and around the church after the bomb went off was also characteristic of dynamite. One investigator, FBI agent John McCormick, said he always got headaches when he was near dynamite explosions; when he arrived at the church, he reported, he immediately experienced the same symptoms. Explosives experts estimated that between ten and twenty sticks of dynamite had been used to create the bomb at the Sixteenth Street church.

In another community, the mere use of dynamite might have provided an important clue. Along with other explosives, dynamite was tightly regulated in many parts of the United States, and some towns and states severely limited the places where dynamite sticks could be purchased. In these communities, FBI agents might profitably have made inquiries at stores

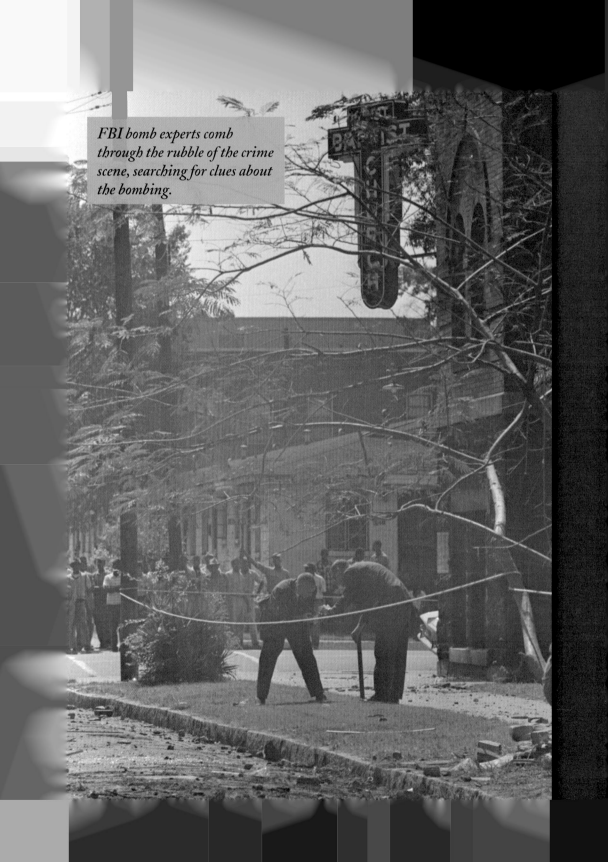

FBI bomb experts comb through the rubble of the crime scene, searching for clues about the bombing.

licensed to sell the explosives, eventually putting together a list of people who had recently purchased dynamite. They then could have questioned each person on the list, perhaps finding the criminal in the process.

In Birmingham, however, dynamite was very easy to find. Though it was technically against the law to own sticks of dynamite without a permit, the reality was that dynamite was everywhere and used for almost every imaginable purpose. "Miners use it," reported a journalist. "Contractors use it. . . . Farmers blow stumps with it, farm kids learn to fish in the creek with dynamite when they are about 13."[20] Dynamite sticks were for sale in dozens of stores throughout the region. The use of dynamite, then, revealed nothing of value to the investigation.

By the Numbers

15

Probable number of sticks of dynamite that caused the explosion

The Crime Scene

Investigators began their survey of the crime scene by confirming parishioners' initial impressions of where the bomb had been planted. The explosion had caused the greatest destruction along the northeastern wall of the church, near the lower-level women's restroom. There, the force of the blast had ripped through a wall 30 inches (76cm) thick, completely torn apart the concrete staircase outside the wall, and leveled the restroom on the other side. In other areas of the building, the damage had been much less severe. The conclusion was clear: The bomb had been placed under the exterior staircase just opposite the women's restroom.

But beyond the location of the explosion, investigators were unable to learn much from the crime scene. The explosion had simply been too powerful. Along with walls, benches, and windows, the blast had destroyed nearly every trace of the original dynamite. Agents found only a small length of wire attached to a fragment of red plastic, which they identified as

By the Numbers

5

days between the integration of Birmingham's public schools and the church bombing

probably a part of a bobber, a small floating object used in fishing. The information was not enough to determine how the bomb had been built—or who had put it together.

The fishing bobber, however, did tell FBI bomb experts that the explosive had probably included a timing device. Such a device prevents a bomb from detonating until a certain period of time has passed. With a timer, a bomber can place an explosive and be long gone from the scene of the crime by the time the bomb actually goes off. Timers are not difficult to make and can frequently be fashioned from ordinary household materials. In fact, several FBI agents had seen timing devices that included fishing bobbers much like the one discovered at the church.

If the bobber was part of a timing device, then the investigation into the bombing had suddenly become much more complex. No longer would agents be looking for a bomber who had necessarily been on the scene at the time of the blast. By using a timer, the bomber could theoretically have placed the explosives earlier on the morning of September 15, or the night before—or perhaps even before that. There was no way to be sure. In the end, the bobber raised more questions than it answered.

Interviews

With physical evidence lacking, investigators turned to other strategies to solve the case. One of these methods, common in police investigations, was interviewing potential witnesses. There had been dozens of people inside the church when the bomb went off, and several others had been standing on the sidewalk, parked in nearby cars, or shopping in various businesses across the street from the bomb site. Investigators hoped that one or more of these people might have observed suspicious activity at some point during the morning.

Because the bomb might have included a timing device, however, investigators could not limit their interviews to those who had been on the scene when the explosion actually took place. They also searched for people who had been near the church earlier that morning or the previous night. Investigators also asked church employees and residents of the neighborhood to describe any unusual happenings in and around the church during the previous few weeks as well. No detail was unimportant, agents assured the people they interviewed. Any event even slightly out of the ordinary could help in solving the crime.

Emergency workers wheel out a covered body from the crime scene.

As is usual in criminal investigations, most of those interviewed had little of importance to report. Few witnesses had noticed anything unusual until the moment the bomb had gone off. To everyone in the building, the explosion had come as a complete shock. No one had noticed any sign of dynamite; no one had seen a mysterious stranger lurking near the northeastern wall of the church. About a dozen people had climbed the exterior staircase that morning, passing within a few feet of the bomb's presumed location, but not a single one had seen the bomb. If a timing device had been used, investigators concluded, the explosives had been well hidden.

Mysterious Cars

But a handful of witnesses did have potentially useful information to report. Shortly after 9:00 on that Sunday morning, while driving to the Sixteenth Street Baptist Church, Mamie and William Grier had seen a greenish Chevrolet that they thought dated from the mid-1950s. The car, they noticed, was equipped with a long radio antenna. At the end of the antenna was a Confederate flag—a prosegregation symbol that was an unusual sight in this heavily black area of Birmingham.

The presence of the flag captured the attention of the Griers, and they decided to follow the car as it made its way through the neighborhood. Their curiosity was heightened when the Chevrolet's driver, a lone white man, turned onto Sixteenth Street and slowly drove in front of their church. But the driver did not stop, and the Griers elected not to pursue him any further. While there was absolutely no evidence connecting the driver to the bombing, the presence of a white man in the area around the church that morning was of great interest to investigators.

Another intriguing lead came from an African American man named James Edward Lay. When racial tensions had risen in Birmingham earlier in the decade, some members of the city's black community had begun patrolling black neighborhoods to guard against Klan activity. Lay, a member of this

Identification of Suspects

When an eyewitness claims to have seen a possible suspect in a criminal case, the following procedure may be used:

1 **Investigators have witnesses** describe the suspect from memory.

2 **In some cases, a police artist,** often with the help of a computer, uses the description to create a sketch of the suspect; the witness can suggest changes in the drawing until the match is as close as possible.

3 **The witness is shown** photographs of various people, including several who resemble the description the witness has given.

4 **The witness points out** any photographs that seem to resemble the suspect and indicates how certain he or she is that the photo depicts the suspect.

group, had been on regular patrol duty during the early morning hours of September 2, just two weeks before the bombing. While driving along Sixteenth Street that night, he told FBI agents, he had noticed a black Ford parked along the northeastern wall of the church building.

There was nothing unusual about a parked car in that area, even at that time of night. But when Lay noticed that the two men in the car were white, he became suspicious. According to Lay, the car's passenger abruptly got out of the Ford, a bag in his hand, and began to walk toward the exterior steps where the bomb had exploded on September 15. When Lay flashed his car's headlights, though, the man ducked back into the Ford and the driver quickly pulled away from the curb. It seemed plausible that Lay had interrupted an earlier attempt to set a bomb at the church—and that the same men had returned two weeks later to try again.

Two More Witnesses

A third eyewitness account also intrigued the FBI. Immediately after the bombing, a black man named John Cunningham was driving near Sixteenth Street when he saw two white men hurrying along a sidewalk. According to Cunningham's account, the two appeared out of breath and frightened. "Those are the bombers,"[21] Cunningham shouted. Stopping the car, he and

Shards of glass and debris litter the altar and the church floor after the explosion.

his passenger jumped out to give chase. But they were too late; the white men were gone.

Perhaps the most valuable eyewitness lead, though, came from a Detroit woman named Kirthus Glenn (whose first name is sometimes given as Gertrude in accounts of the case). In the days before the bombing, Glenn had come to Birmingham to visit friends who lived in a house near the Sixteenth Street church. At about 2:10 on the morning of the 15th, she told FBI officials, she was driving to her friends' home from another part of town when she noticed a car parked near the church building. There were three, possibly four men in the car, Glenn reported, and though she got a good look at only one of them—a man in the back seat—she could tell that all of them were white. The car quickly drove off when Glenn pulled into a nearby parking spot.

The incident worried Glenn. As an FBI summary of her statement put it, she knew that it was rare to see whites in a neighborhood almost exclusively "occupied by members of the Negro race."[22] It was even odder to see three or four white men simply sitting in a car in this all-black neighborhood. And the late hour, of course, made the situation all the more peculiar—and all the more suspicious.

Glenn was sufficiently disturbed to study the car carefully in the few seconds before the driver pulled away. Later, she recalled the vehicle as a mid-1950s turquoise Chevrolet with a long radio antenna on the left rear fender. "They must have a phone in there,"[23] she remembered telling her passenger half-jokingly. Although the vehicle Glenn had seen had no Confederate flag on its antenna, it otherwise matched the vehicle Mamie and William Grier said they had seen cruising the streets around the church some seven hours later.

Thomas Blanton

The stories of these eyewitnesses were not perfect. None of the witnesses had gotten a close look at the white men they had seen near the Sixteenth Street Baptist Church. Kirthus Glenn

Thomas Blanton Jr. arrives at the Jefferson County courthouse in 2001 to stand trial for his involvement in the 1963 church bombing.

had perhaps had the best view of any of the witnesses, but even she saw the face of the man in the rear seat of the Chevrolet from a distance, at night, and only briefly. No witness had seen the white men planting a bomb—or, for that matter, committing any kind of crime. The suspicions of the witnesses rested almost entirely on the presence of white men in what was ordinarily an all-black part of town.

Still, the eyewitnesses had offered some important leads—especially when FBI agents realized that one local Klan member, Thomas Blanton Jr., owned a car that looked very much like the one described by Kirthus Glenn and the Griers. Blanton's car was blue, rather than turquoise, as Glenn had described it, or green, which had been the Griers' impression. But it was a Chevrolet dating from the mid-1950s, and it had a long, whiplike antenna. Better yet, when Glenn was shown pictures of several different cars and asked to indicate whether the one she had seen was among them, she unhesitatingly pointed to the photo of Blanton's vehicle.

Nor was Blanton's car the only clue that indicated his involvement in the bombing. Though Glenn could not identify Blanton—he was evidently not the man she had seen in the rear seat—two other witnesses thought that they might have seen the Klansman near the church. After viewing pictures of possible suspects, James Lay reported that Blanton, or someone who looked very much like him, had carried a bag up to the steps of the church on the night of September 2. John Cunningham, likewise, had gotten a quick look at one of the two men he had observed running away from the church just after the explosion. While he could not be sure he had seen Blanton, the account Cunningham gave of this man matched Blanton's general description.

More Questions

The evidence against Blanton was sketchy, to be sure. Even if the car was his, someone else could have been driving it. Likewise, there were probably dozens of men in and around

FBI Informers

Gary Thomas Rowe, who provided the FBI with information about the workings of the Ku Klux Klan in and around Birmingham, was only one of many Klan informers used by the bureau during the 1960s. The FBI has released few records of the scope of its attempt to infiltrate the Klan, but modern estimates of the number of Klan informers during this period range from a few dozen to several hundred. Many of these no doubt passed on information only occasionally. Rowe and some others, however, spoke frequently with FBI agents.

The informers were certainly valuable in identifying Klan members and in alerting federal officials to the activities of local Klan organizations. Nonetheless, the hiring of informers was controversial. One reason involved the violent nature of the Klan itself. In theory, informers such as Rowe were expected to avoid taking part in fighting and other acts of cruelty. In practice, however, this was not always possible; an informer who routinely declined to participate in violence would stand out as a spy. The FBI thus found itself in the uncomfortable position of paying people who were violating laws.

Moreover, the FBI's need to protect its informants sometimes appeared to overshadow its desire to solve crimes. In several cases in which Klan members were accused of violence, FBI officials moved slowly to avoid compromising the cover of their informers. And in a few cases, observers and historians have charged that FBI agents deliberately suppressed evidence that their informers had been involved in murders or other exceptionally violent acts. Whether these charges are true remains a topic for debate, but it cannot be denied that the practice of paying informers made the FBI vulnerable to such charges.

Birmingham who fit the description given by Lay and Cunningham. Still, if the witnesses could be believed, Blanton had been at the scene of the crime just after the bomb exploded—and he, or at least his car, had been in the area at least twice during the previous eight hours. There was no question that Blanton was a prime suspect in the case.

In reality, though, investigators already had their eyes on Blanton and would have suspected him regardless of the eyewitness accounts. Even by the standards of the Ku Klux Klan, Blanton seemed particularly angry, violent, and prejudiced. Though only in his mid-twenties, Blanton had been suspected several times of violence against blacks and other minority groups. Upon learning that a neighbor was Catholic, for instance, Blanton had vandalized her car and thrown rocks at her home. As an FBI investigator put it, Blanton had a "history of psychopathic behavior."[24]

Moreover, through their informer Gary Thomas Rowe, FBI agents learned that Blanton had recently withdrawn from his klavern. In meetings throughout the summer of 1963, Blanton had spoken in favor of stepping up violence against blacks, especially against those who agitated for civil rights. When others cautioned him to wait, Blanton announced the formation of a new and more extreme Klan chapter, to be known as the Cahaba Boys. Rowe claimed not to know the specifics of Blanton's plans, but he did tell FBI agents that several other local Klansmen had eagerly joined Blanton as members of the new splinter group.

Klan member Robert Chambliss was immediately suspected of involvement in the church bombing.

Robert Chambliss

One of the new Cahaba Boys was a man named Robert Chambliss. Though Chambliss, at fifty-nine, was much older than Thomas

Blanton, the two men were kindred spirits. Known as "Dynamite Bob" within the Klan community, Chambliss had knowledge of explosives and—so it was rumored—plenty of experience using them against blacks. He had been a chief suspect in several of the bombing cases preceding the blast at the Sixteenth Street Baptist Church. Many observers believed, moreover, that Chambliss had been involved in bombings, beatings, and other acts of terror against Birmingham's blacks for at least the previous twenty years.

As with Blanton, Chambliss's personality and history of violence led investigators to put him on their short list of possible suspects. But FBI agents also used the eyewitness account of Kirthus Glenn to focus their investigation on Chambliss. Not long after the bombing, an FBI employee showed Glenn more than thirty photos of known Klansmen and asked her to point to those that showed the man in the back seat of the car she had seen early in the morning of September 15. Without hesitation, Glenn picked out three photos. Each depicted Chambliss.

Glenn's identification of Chambliss, of course, did not provide convincing proof that he was the man in the back of the car. The hour was late; the light was bad. And even if the man had been Chambliss, Glenn had not seen him actually doing anything illegal. Still, though the evidence against Chambliss and Blanton was imperfect, it pointed the way. FBI agents had a clear direction for their investigation. They now hoped to find evidence that would prove their case against the two men— and anyone who had assisted them.

CHAPTER 3

The Investigation Stalls

By late September 1963, FBI agents were focusing much of their attention on Blanton and Chambliss. At the same time, they had begun a close investigation of Bobby Frank Cherry and Troy Ingram, two other members of the Cahaba Boys. Cherry was the man described by historian Diane McWhorter as having no front teeth, an eighth-grade education, and a fondness for beating his wife; years later, Cherry's son Tom would say that his father had joined the Klan because "it made him feel like a big fish in a small pond."[25] Ingram, from a similar background, was of particular interest to investigators because he had recently broken a toe. Witness John Cunningham had reported that one of the men he had seen on the sidewalk after the bombing had been limping; federal agents speculated that Ingram might have been that man.

Exactly what took place on the night of September 14 and the morning of the 15th was still very much open to question, but FBI officials were developing a theory. As they saw it, the bomb had been created by some combination of the four men they suspected most strongly—Chambliss, Blanton, Ingram, and Cherry—perhaps with the help of other local Klansmen, notably truck driver John Wesley Hall, laborer Charles Cagle, and Herman Cash, whose brother Jack owned a restaurant that served as a frequent Klan meeting spot. At about 2:00 on the morning of September 15, investigators speculated, the chief suspects had driven to the church in Blanton's car, concealed the bomb beneath the stairs, and driven home immediately after Kirthus Glenn had parked her own vehicle.

Investigators believed that the bomb had most likely been set to go off sometime during the night, before worship services

Bobby Frank Cherry was added to the FBI's list of suspects shortly after the bombing.

began; this pattern would have been consistent with earlier bombings. When the dynamite failed to explode by dawn, agents suspected, Blanton had become curious. He returned to the church at 9:00, when the Griers had sighted his car, and again—this time with Ingram—just after 10:00. Blanton and Ingram had still been in the neighborhood at 10:22, investigators supposed, and while hurrying back to their vehicle had been spotted by John Cunningham. The theory was only a theory. But it did fit the facts.

"I Was at Home"

FBI agents subjected their suspects to repeated interviews, hoping that they would contradict themselves, implicate each other, or—better yet—confess. Again and again, however, the suspects proclaimed their innocence. "I was at home when [the bombing] happened, I reckon,"[26] Chambliss told one investigator, and he produced several relatives who swore that he had been in and around his house the entire morning of the 15th. Blanton, in turn, said that he had been out with a girlfriend, Jean Casey, on the evening of the 14th and had been nowhere near the church at any point during the night. Ingram and Cherry also claimed to have been elsewhere during the time period in question.

The suspects were happy to respond to other lines of questioning. All freely admitted to being racists. Some even admitted a willingness to use violence against blacks, at least in certain circumstances. "I would kill a nigger if he bothered me,"[27] Cherry told an investigator. Most acknowledged past ties to the Ku Klux Klan, though only Cherry owned up to being a current member. But each man consistently claimed to know nothing about the church bombing. Indeed, they all

By the Numbers

1

Arrests made by federal agents during the 1960s in connection with the bombing case expressed disgust at the deaths of the four girls. If he knew who had set off the bomb, Blanton assured investigators, he "would identify them without hesitation."[28]

Despite their apparent willingness to cooperate with investigators, the suspects did at times grow frustrated with the continual questioning. "Everywhere we went, the FBI was already there waiting for us, wanting to talk,"[29] recalled one Klansman years later. Occasionally, the attention caused the suspects to lose their tempers. "Stay away from my house and don't talk to my wife and relatives any more," a furious Chambliss once snapped at a pair of officers. "I'm warning you."[30] Blanton even ended one interview by attacking a federal agent. But investigators welcomed these reactions. An angry, out-of-control suspect, agents knew, was more likely to divulge useful information than one who remained calm and rational throughout an interview.

A Cover-up?

In the first week or so after the bombing, federal investigators seemed to be free to handle the case as they saw fit. As the days passed, however, some of the South's more enthusiastic segregationists began challenging the FBI's interpretation of events. These people argued that the explosion might not have been the work of white racists at all. Instead, they argued, the bombing could have been carried out by blacks hoping to encourage sympathy for their cause. "The Negroes," theorized influential Georgia senator Richard B. Russell, "might have perpetrated this incident in order to keep emotions at a fever pitch."[31]

FBI officials never seriously believed that black activists had set off the bomb. But laying the rumors to rest proved almost impossible. When a federal official denied that the bombing had been the work of civil rights advocates, many Alabamians simply ignored him. Others suspected that the FBI was ignoring evidence that did not suit its bias against segregationists. One newspaper editor spoke for many white south-

Blaming the Victims

The widespread belief among white southerners that blacks, not whites, were responsible for the church bombing had counterparts in other cases, too. In the so-called Mississippi Burning case, for example, three civil rights workers vanished one June evening in 1964. Though federal agents immediately suspected that the three men had been killed by white supremacists, several weeks went by without any evidence proving this theory. As time passed, more and more southern whites charged that the men had run away of their own accord; their apparent disappearance was only a hoax, designed to play up the supposed violence of white Mississippians. In this view, the three missing workers were safe and in hiding—and enjoying the attention the national media was paying to the problems of blacks in Mississippi. Later that summer, however, the corpses of the three missing men were found, putting an end to this type of speculation.

erners when he charged that the federal government was "trying to cover up any clues to the crime that may damage the Negro cause."[32]

Three Arrests

The relationship between the FBI and the whites of Alabama soon became even more tenuous. Just two weeks after the explosion, Alabama law enforcement officers arrested Robert Chambliss, along with fellow Klansmen Charles Cagle and John Wesley Hall, on charges related to the bombing. But the charges had nothing to do with murder. Nor had Alabama seen fit to arrest the three Klan members for setting off explosives, for damaging property, or for injuring innocent people. Instead, the state accused the Klansmen of a minor, seldom-enforced, and ultimately rather trivial offense: illegal possession of dynamite.

FBI leaders were furious when they heard the news. J. Edgar Hoover accused state officials of deliberately compromising the bureau's investigation into the bombing. By arresting the three men on these minor charges, Hoover complained, the state had tipped off the Klan that federal investigators were close to learning the truth. In this way, Hoover believed, the arrests served to warn local Klansmen to be more careful in their dealings with federal agents. "From now on," writes historian Gary May, summing up Hoover's view of the situation, "Klansmen would hire lawyers and keep their mouths shut."[33]

Former Klan member Mitchell Burns, pictured in 2001, taped private Klan conversations for the FBI during the investigation.

Civil rights leaders were angry, too. To them, the arrests were yet another sign that state and local police forces were not to be trusted. By charging the men with nothing more serious than possession of dynamite, activists lamented, the state police had trivialized the lives of the girls who died in the bombing. And when Chambliss was acquitted and all charges

were dropped against Cagle and Hall, movement leaders were enraged. Like Hoover and his agents, civil rights advocates concluded that the arrests had been designed not to punish the bombers, but to protect them—and to confuse the federal effort to gather evidence against the killers. "It was a farce,"[34] fumed one of Martin Luther King's assistants.

Protecting the Bombers

In any case, the charges lodged against Cagle, Hall, and Chambliss presented a problem for the FBI. At the very least, the arrests showed that state and local officials were deeply hostile toward federal involvement in the case. State officers had refused to share information or discuss strategy with FBI agents; the arrests had come as a complete surprise to FBI officials. Moreover, Alabama officials gloated that they had moved speedily to "solve" the case while federal agents were continuing to plod away. "We certainly beat the Kennedy crowd to the punch,"[35] crowed Wallace, referring not only to the president, John Kennedy, but also to the president's brother, U.S. attorney general Robert Kennedy. And by warning the Klansmen of the dangers they faced, the arrests had put the bombers on guard.

At the time, FBI officials strongly suspected that the problem went even deeper. Some state and local law enforcement agents, they believed, were not only sympathetic to the Klan, but were working directly with Klan members to protect the bombers. Later research by historians such as Birmingham native Diane McWhorter confirms this view. Shortly before the arrests of Cagle, Chambliss, and Hall, McWhorter writes, several Klansmen were called to a secret meeting with Al Lingo, Alabama's director of public safety. At this meeting, according to McWhorter, Lingo warned the Klansmen that the FBI was making progress, outlined the plan to arrest the three men on dynamite charges, and made it clear that the reason for the arrests was to interfere with the FBI's investigation. FBI officials, then, were more accurate than they knew.

Families, Friends, and Neighbors

Still, with or without the cooperation of local agencies, and with or without the statements of local Klansmen, the federal investigation into the church bombing continued. Throughout the fall, FBI officials talked to dozens of family members, friends, and neighbors of the chief suspects in the case. Most of these interviews did little to advance the investigation. Asked about her husband's activities, Troy Ingram's wife explained that her husband was "not the type of person to be involved in violence."[36] Likewise, Jean Casey, Thomas Blanton's girlfriend, confirmed that she had been with him on September 14. Though investigators suspected Casey was lying to protect him, they could not prove their contention.

On the other hand, a few of those interviewed did speak unfavorably of the suspects. "I have heard [Troy Ingram] and others talk about beating up Negroes with chains,"[37] reported one man. In some cases, investigators recruited friends of the suspects to inform against them. Birmingham resident Mitchell Burns, for example, allowed the FBI to place a tape recorder in his car. That allowed the FBI to overhear conversations Burns had while driving with his friends Thomas Blanton and Bobby Frank Cherry. At first, Burns had been reluctant to work with the FBI, but when agents showed him photos of the bodies of the four girls killed in the blast, he changed his mind. "[The bodies] were very mangled," he recalled years later. "It was sickening to look at."[38]

The FBI obtained particularly useful evidence from Robert Chambliss's niece, Elizabeth Cobbs. When they learned that Cobbs disliked and distrusted Chambliss, FBI agents encouraged her to help them gather evidence against her uncle. Knowing that Chambliss had a fierce temper, Cobbs, like Burns, was reluctant to help at first. If her uncle found out that she had been talking to the FBI, she said, he would be "capable of planting a bomb in the middle of [her] house."[39] But when FBI officials promised to keep her identity a secret, Cobbs revealed several intriguing pieces of information.

Becoming a Polygraph Operator

Job Description:
Polygraph operators administer polygraph tests, most often to people who are suspected of criminal misconduct or to job applicants, especially in criminal justice fields. Polygraph operators also interpret the results of these tests.

Education:
Varies. Many polygraph operators are drawn from police departments, so the qualifications of a police officer (which may include, for example, a college degree and police training) apply. In addition, most polygraph operators must attend classes in polygraphy at colleges accredited by the American Polygraph Association.

Qualifications:
Polygraph operators need to have good communication skills, both in speech and in writing. They are required to keep up with interviewing techniques, advances in equipment, and the laws that pertain to polygraph tests.

Additional Information:
Some employers may require additional qualifications or skills. For example, agencies may insist that an applicant pass drug tests, hold a valid driver's license, or pass a background check before being hired.

Salary:
Varies. Many polygraph operators, if not most, administer tests as only a part of their job responsibilities.

The first took place during a conversation on Saturday, September 14. "You just wait 'til after Sunday morning," Chambliss told his niece; then, referring to Birmingham's blacks, he added grimly, "They'll beg us to let them segregate!" Surprised, Cobbs pressed him to explain what he meant. "I've got enough stuff put away to flatten half of Birmingham,"[40] Chambliss replied cryptically. The next morning, when she heard the news of the bombing at the church, Cobbs could not help recalling what her uncle had told her.

Cobbs also reported an interesting remark her uncle had made almost a week after the explosion. On September 21, Cobbs told officials, she was at Chambliss's house when her uncle came into the living room to watch the evening news. The lead story that night was about the bombing. At one point during the broadcast, Cobbs said, Chambliss leaned toward

An FBI agent interprets the results of a polygraph reading for his colleagues as they interrogate a suspect in this 1954 photo.

the screen. "It wasn't meant to hurt anybody," Cobbs remembered her uncle murmuring, as if he were speaking directly to the anchorman. "It didn't go off when it was supposed to."[41] Both these statements, along with a few others, bolstered the FBI's belief that Chambliss had been part of the bombing plot.

Microphones and Polygraphs

Statements from witnesses such as Kirthus Glenn and Elizabeth Cobbs were valuable—not merely for the information these witnesses provided, but also because their evidence could be used in court if Chambliss was to be tried. That was not the case, however, with all the information gathered by federal investigators. In a criminal trial, the source of the evidence against a suspect is of critical importance. Courts have strict rules about what evidence may and may not be introduced at a trial. No matter how helpful a piece of information may be in proving guilt, it must have been obtained according to the guidelines of the criminal justice system. If the rules have not been followed, the evidence will be excluded from the trial.

One such ban involves evidence obtained through the use of bugs, or listening devices. Following the bombing, investigators placed hidden microphones and wiretaps in the homes of Thomas Blanton and other suspects. Some of these bugs secretly recorded telephone conversations; others allowed investigators to hear discussions taking place in various rooms of the house. From time to time, the bugs picked up conversations in which a suspect made an incriminating statement. In a tape made a year or two after the bombing, for instance, Blanton could be heard telling someone else that he and several friends had once constructed a bomb in a secluded area outside Birmingham.

But in 1963, the FBI could not use this type of evidence in court. Agents were allowed to use listening devices only for the purpose of surveillance—that is, for keeping the suspects under close observation. The tapes thus strongly suggested that federal investigators were pursuing the right suspects, but could not help put anyone in jail. In 1968, the law was changed to allow law enforcement agencies to use this kind of evidence in court if a judge agreed to let them place the bugs. In 1963, though, with a few exceptions—notably the conversations recorded in the car belonging to FBI informer Mitchell Burns, conversations that were obtained with Burns's permission—the FBI's tapes could not be introduced at a trial.

FBI officials also were barred from using information they had gathered from polygraph tests. A polygraph, sometimes called a lie detector, measures physical responses to questions. Polygraph technicians ask a subject a list of questions and determine the level of stress for each answer. By examining body functions such as blood pressure, perspiration, and heart rate—all of which often increase dramatically when a subject is under stress—trained technicians claim to be able to tell whether the subject is answering a given question truthfully. Though most observers agree that polygraphs are often very accurate, the devices are not perfect. Rather than convict a defendant based on a possibly incorrect polygraph reading, therefore, courts usually exclude polygraph evidence from trials.

Even so, FBI agents administered polygraph tests to the chief suspects in the case. Many of the results strongly suggested involvement in the bombing. When Blanton was asked whether he was at the Sixteenth Street Baptist Church at 2:00 on the morning of the 15th, for instance, he answered no—but sudden changes in his vital signs suggested that this answer was a lie. Cherry's polygraph indicated that he was keeping evidence from FBI interviewers. Ingram's showed "a classic textbook type pattern of deception across the board."[42] Though the tests would not be usable in court, they reassured FBI personnel that they were looking in the right direction.

Admission of Failure

In spite of the investigative tools at their disposal, however, FBI agents seemed unable to close the case. By the end of 1963, the FBI had made no arrests in the church bombing investi-

Other Civil Rights Cases

During the 1950s and 1960s, it was generally true that southern states did not convict whites of murdering blacks—or white civil rights workers. In 1955, for example, Emmett Till, a teenager from Chicago, was killed in Mississippi after allegedly admiring a white woman he met in a store. Two white defendants were arrested, but an all-white jury quickly acquitted both. Nine years later, in another Mississippi case, FBI agents found the bodies of three missing civil rights workers buried beneath an earthen dam in a rural part of the state. Several Klan members were

The bodies of three missing Mississippi civil rights workers are discovered beneath an earthen dam in 1964.

eventually convicted of conspiring to deprive the three men of their civil rights, a charge with a maximum penalty of ten years in prison. At the time, none of these men was charged with murder.

Refusal to convict whites for race-based murder was not limited to Mississippi. In 1965, white civil rights advocate Viola Liuzzo journeyed to Alabama from her home in Michigan to assist the movement. One of her tasks was to drive black protesters back and forth between the cities of Selma and Montgomery. On one of these trips, Liuzzo was shot and killed. As in the Mississippi case the year before, Alabama officials successfully prosecuted three white Klan members in connection with the crime—but charged them only with conspiracy, not murder.

By the Numbers

0

Murder charges filed during the 1960s in connection with the case

gation. As 1964 began, Hoover kept up the pressure on the Klansmen. Agents continued to swarm around Birmingham; investigators recruited new informers—including John Wesley Hall, one of the men arrested by state officials on dynamite charges— and returned again and again to talk to the chief suspects and those who knew them. Yet 1964 passed without any charges being filed, and so did 1965. By 1968, five years after the bombing, it was clear that the FBI would not be charging anyone in connection with the case.

The failure to prosecute was not based on a lack of information. Tapes, polygraph results, eyewitness accounts, and other evidence all led to the same conclusion: The bombing had been carried out by Chambliss, Blanton, Cherry, and probably Troy Ingram and Herman Cash. In 1965, FBI agents in Birmingham sent Hoover these five names and informed him that the case was as good as solved. "No avenue of investigative inquiry has been overlooked,"[43] the agents pointed out.

Secretive as always, Hoover never gave any specific reason for failing to prosecute. Some historians have speculated that Hoover's distaste for the civil rights movement made him reluctant to bring the bombers to justice. Others have suggested that FBI informant Gary Thomas Rowe might have been peripherally involved in the bombing and that Hoover ended the investigation in order to cover up Rowe's participation. There may be some truth to both these theories. On the other hand, Hoover's hostility toward civil rights leaders was matched by his hostility toward the Ku Klux Klan, and the energy the FBI put into the church bombing case suggests that Hoover dearly wanted to solve the crime.

The problems with the FBI's evidence provide a more plausible explanation of Hoover's decision to drop the case.

Polygraph data was inadmissible in court, as was the information obtained through most of the listening devices, and there was virtually no usable evidence from the crime scene. As a result, the case against the Cahaba Boys rested largely on brief descriptions of suspicious behavior. No witness had seen the men build the bomb. No one saw the bombers light the fuse. No physical evidence connected the suspects with the explosion. Jurors might believe the accounts of witnesses such as Elizabeth Cobbs and Kirthus Glenn—but then again, they might not.

And given what he knew of Birmingham in the mid-1960s, Hoover strongly suspected that jurors in the case would not. Because of the racism that permeated the city and the mistrust that marked white Alabamians' response to the federal investigators, Hoover was convinced that no Alabama jury would convict white men of murdering black children. In some other time or place, he reasoned, it might have made sense to arrest the suspects and bring them to trial. In Alabama of the early 1960s, however, Hoover believed that bringing this case to court would be a waste of time. "The chance of successful prosecution," he wrote to an aide, "is very remote."[44] The search for the Birmingham church bombers had apparently come to an end.

CHAPTER 4

Reopening the Case

By the early 1970s, many Americans had more or less forgotten the bombing of the Sixteenth Street Baptist Church. In 1963, the tragedy had captured the attention of the nation and drawn all eyes toward Birmingham. But now, the bombing seemed a relic of another time. New disasters, new social movements, and new controversies had sprung up to replace the bombing in the popular mind. Few paid much heed to the deaths of four girls in an explosion nearly ten years before.

Still, even long after the bombing, some Americans recalled the events of that September morning in 1963 with great clarity. The surviving relatives of Cynthia Wesley, Addie Mae Collins, Carole Robertson, and Denise McNair, of course, would never forget what happened on that tragic day. Neither would most people who had known the girls and their parents. "The bombing . . . will forever be in my memory,"[45] noted U.S. secretary of state Condoleezza Rice more than forty years after the tragedy; as a girl, Rice had been a friend of Denise McNair. And whether they were acquainted with the families or not, many people who had been active in the civil rights movement at that time felt the same way.

Bill Baxley

But clear memories of the explosion were not limited to African Americans, or to civil rights leaders, or to the friends and families of the four victims. Another person who never forgot the case was a white man named Bill Baxley, who had been a law student at the University of Alabama during the fall of 1963. When he heard about the explosion, he recalled years afterward, "it just made me sick.. . . I wondered who could do something

In the 1970s Alabama's attorney general Bill Baxley reopened the investigation into the church bombing.

By the Numbers

4

Years between Baxley's request for information from the FBI and the granting of his request

like that, kill four kids."[46] Baxley followed the investigation into the crime with great interest and was disgusted when the FBI failed to prosecute. Hoping to begin a career in government and politics, Baxley vowed to do whatever he could to avenge the deaths of the four girls.

In 1970, seven years after the bombing of the church, Baxley won election as attorney general, or chief prosecutor, of Alabama. In this post, Baxley was responsible for bringing criminal charges against those who broke Alabama's laws. One of his first acts in office was to reopen the church bombing case—that is, to reexamine the evidence with an eye toward possibly making arrests. Baxley noted that all five of the FBI's chief suspects—Chambliss, Blanton, Ingram, Cherry, and Cash—were still living in the Birmingham area and that not one was in prison for the crime of killing the four girls in 1963. "This case," he told an associate, "is going to be [my] number one priority."[47]

Baxley's eagerness to revive the bombing case was motivated largely by a desire to see justice done. But he also believed that the people of Birmingham were ready for the case to be reopened. Alabama, he noted, was no longer as segregationist as it had once been. By now the state's black citizens voted, went to college, and served on juries alongside whites. While racism was by no means dead, it was not nearly as virulent as it had been in 1963. Should the case be brought to trial, Baxley argued, local whites would now be able to judge the case on its merits, rather than simply voting to acquit all white defendants regardless of the evidence.

In early 1971, shortly after taking office, Baxley formed a task force of lawyers and investigators and set them to work on the bombing case. Before long, it became apparent that much of the information the team needed was contained in the FBI files. Accordingly, Baxley asked the FBI for copies of what the

Fred Shuttlesworth

Fred Shuttlesworth, an advocate for nonviolent protest, holds a press conference shortly after the church bombing.

The most famous person associated with the civil rights movement in Birmingham was Martin Luther King Jr. But Fred Shuttlesworth may have been the single most important figure in the local movement. Shuttlesworth, the minister of Birmingham's Bethel Baptist Church, was a cofounder of at least two civil rights organizations. He was also instrumental in organizing protests and demonstrations in Birmingham. Shuttlesworth had sued the city to open its park system to blacks as well as whites and had led an ultimately successful fight to desegregate the buses.

Shuttlesworth paid dearly for his activism. White supremacists bombed his home not once but twice. When he tried to enroll his daughter in an all-white public school—supported in part by the taxes he paid—angry whites met him at the school entrance and whipped him with a chain. Later, during a protest during the summer of 1963, police officers pinned him against a wall with a blast from a fire hose. Nonetheless, Shuttlesworth continued to fight, and he never lost hope for the movement he had helped to begin. "If you win in Birmingham," he told his supporters, "as Birmingham goes, so goes the nation."

Quoted in Henry Hampton and Steve Fayer, *Voices of Freedom.* New York: Bantam, 1990, p. 125.

agency had collected. But J. Edgar Hoover denied repeated requests, and when Hoover died in 1972, his successor, Clarence Kelley, did the same. Not until 1975 did federal officials finally agree to allow Baxley's task force to examine the agency's files.

Even then, Baxley and his staffers were not allowed access to every piece of information the FBI had gathered. For reasons that remain unclear today, Baxley's investigators were never told, for example, that agents had taped Klansmen's conversations during the 1960s. FBI officials refused to release certain documents that might have revealed the identities of bureau informers, and many of the documents the agency did release had key names blacked out. Finally, the files made heavy use of aliases and code names, such as "Abingdon Spaulding" for Chambliss's niece Elizabeth Cobbs. But even with some information missing or unavailable, sorting through the remaining files still took months.

Bob Eddy

By late 1976, during the middle of Baxley's second term in office, the task force's study of the FBI files was at last complete. The following January, the investigation into the bombing began in earnest. Baxley entrusted the reopening of the case to a law enforcement agent named Bob Eddy. "I want you to go to Birmingham," Baxley instructed Eddy. "I want you to go there and read everything you can on the case. I want you to talk to everyone you can—FBI, police, klansmen, people at the church."[48]

Eddy and several other agents began by interviewing and reinterviewing people with connections to the case. Most of these people, as Eddy expected, added little to the investigators' understanding of what had happened at the church on September 15. Many repeated substantially the same stories that they had told FBI investigators more than a decade earlier. Some said they had never known much about the case to begin with; others had forgotten details over the years. As Elizabeth Cobbs wryly noted in a book written years after the reopening of the case, Eddy and his staff came to expect that every discussion would be "just another 'I don't know anything, I didn't see anything' interview."[49]

In some cases, Eddy and his staff believed that their interview subjects really did have nothing to add. At times, though, they thought otherwise. The Ku Klux Klan had declined in membership and visibility in the fourteen years since the bombing, but the organization still had a powerful hold over at least some of the witnesses he interviewed. Many, Eddy believed, continued to adhere to a Klan code of silence. Others, he thought, feared reprisals from the Klan if it became known that they were talking to the state agents. Eddy did his best to encourage these men to discuss the case freely with his staff, but most simply refused.

Building a Case

Of the five chief suspects in the church bombing case, Eddy soon realized, one appeared to stand out. More than Thomas Blanton, more than Herman Cash, more than Troy Ingram, who had died in 1973, and more than Bobby Frank Cherry, the name of Robert Chambliss seemed to come up again and again. Chambliss had a long history of violence and an easy familiarity with explosives. According to several witnesses, he had played important roles in earlier bombings, including a 1958 attack on the home of black minister and civil rights activist Fred Shuttlesworth, though Chambliss had never been charged with

Robert Chambliss (second from left), a prime suspect in Bob Eddy's investigation, confers with his lawyers in 1977.

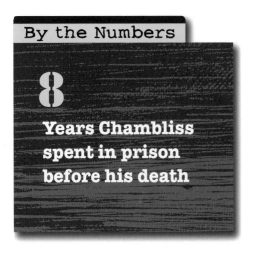

8

Years Chambliss spent in prison before his death

crimes in these incidents either. As Eddy saw it, Chambliss seemed to be at the very center of the case.

Moreover, Eddy believed, the evidence against Chambliss was much stronger than the evidence implicating Cherry, Cash, or Blanton. Kirthus Glenn had confidently identified Chambliss as the man she had seen outside the Sixteenth Street Baptist Church early on the morning of September 15. Elizabeth Cobbs had reported several incriminating statements Chambliss had made to her both before and after the bombing. To the best of Eddy's knowledge, no other suspect had been recognized so clearly by an eyewitness, and no other suspect had made so many unguarded remarks. Accordingly, Eddy decided to focus the investigation primarily on Chambliss.

Eddy began by making contact with Elizabeth Cobbs, now a Methodist minister in her late thirties and still living in the Birmingham area. Cobbs was willing to talk to investigators, and she freely admitted her continuing dislike for Chambliss. However, she told Eddy, she would not agree to testify against her uncle should the case come to court. Her refusal stemmed mainly from her fear of Chambliss and the possibility of violent revenge from him if she spoke out publicly. Such violence was especially likely, Cobbs believed, if Chambliss was found not guilty on all charges. "Acquittal," she wrote, "would have meant a very sure death sentence for me and perhaps for [family members] I could not protect."[50]

Cobbs's decision also rested on her negative experiences with the FBI during the 1960s. By cooperating with the FBI investigation at that time, Cobbs believed that she had put herself at great personal risk. She had feared that her uncle would learn of her cooperation with the FBI, but at the time, she had trusted that Chambliss would soon be sent to jail for his part in the bombing. When J. Edgar Hoover elected not to press charges against Chambliss and the other suspects, however, Cobbs had experienced a deep sense of betrayal. "I felt as used and abused as it is possible for a person to feel," she wrote years later. "All the intrigue, all the real and perceived danger, all the risk of discovery . . . for nothing. Absolutely nothing."[51]

Baxley and Eddy spent much of August 1977 trying to persuade Cobbs to change her mind. They appealed to her sense of justice and her hatred of her uncle, and they focused on the grim results of the bombing. "Four kids were killed,"[52] Baxley emphasized during one meeting. When Cobbs expressed fear that Chambliss might exact revenge on her if she testified, Baxley promised police protection for her and her family. He and Eddy also gently reminded her that the power of the Klan was not what it had been in 1963. Still, by the end of August, Cobbs had not yet agreed to testify.

Kirthus Glenn

While Eddy and Baxley were encouraging Cobbs to speak out against her uncle, other members of the task force traveled to Detroit to talk to Kirthus Glenn. Glenn seemed pleased to see the investigators and was delighted that one of the supposed bombers might be put on trial. But like Cobbs, she refused to take part in a court case. Glenn told agents that she worried for her safety and did not wish to leave her home for an extended period of time. Even a personal visit by Baxley to Detroit could not change her mind.

Returning to Birmingham, Baxley made a last-ditch effort to gain Glenn's participation. More than twenty years earlier, in 1955, a black civil rights advocate named Rosa Parks had made headlines by refusing to give a white man her seat on a city bus in Montgomery, Alabama's capital city. Her decision, which helped to spark the civil rights movement across the South, had led to her arrest. She was represented in court by a black lawyer named Fred Gray. Hoping that Glenn might agree to testify if Gray, a noted star of the civil rights struggle, encouraged her to do so, Baxley called Gray and asked for his help.

A few days later, Gray and Baxley flew to Detroit to meet with Glenn. Together, the two men described the progress of the civil rights movement in the South since 1963 and spoke of the need to exorcise the ghosts of the past by convicting

Becoming an Attorney General

Job Description:
Each state has its own attorney general, and the federal government has one as well. Attorneys general are the chief prosecutors of their government. It is the attorney general's job to oversee the prosecution from start to finish: to gather the evidence needed to solve crimes, to file charges against the suspects, and to argue the case at trial.

Education:
Attorneys general are lawyers, so they must have completed college, graduated from an accredited law school, and passed their state's bar exam.

Qualifications:
Many states, such as Alabama and New York, choose their attorney general through direct election. Other states, including Wyoming, allow the governor to appoint an attorney general; this is the method used on the federal level as well.

Additional Information:
States may establish additional requirements for the office of attorney general. In Alabama, for example, the attorney general must be at least twenty-five, must have been an Alabama resident for at least five years, and must have been a U. S. citizen for at least seven years.

Salary:
Set by the state legislature or U.S. Congress; usually $50,000 and up.

those who had taken part in the church bombing. After listening closely, Glenn at last agreed to testify. Delighted, Baxley promised that the state of Alabama would pay all Glenn's expenses and provide her with any police protection she needed. He flew back to Birmingham in triumph. One of his best witnesses was willing to take part in the trial. The next step was to convince Elizabeth Cobbs to testify as well.

The Last Witness

In her next meeting with Eddy, however, Cobbs simply repeated her earlier unwillingness to talk. As she had told investigators earlier, she feared for her safety and the safety of her family. Moreover, she could not shake the suspicion that Baxley and Eddy were not truly serious about bringing charges against her uncle. "It might just be another political show to appear to be doing something for votes,"[53] she remembered thinking. Cobbs continued to suspect that this investigation would be just like the FBI's: a great deal of stress and no visible result.

But as she continued to meet with Eddy and his agents, Cobbs began to change her thinking. She began to realize the value of the information she had. It gradually became apparent to her that Chambliss probably could not be convicted without her testimony, that her accounts of what Chambliss had said and done were central to a successful prosecution of the case. Cobbs also came to see just how furious she was at her uncle, not only for the church bombing but also for the way he had treated her and other family members over the years. "I wanted the horror put to rest," she wrote afterward. "I wanted Robert, who I knew to be a human monster, to face a penalty for his crimes."[54] In early September, at last, Cobbs agreed to testify.

A Visit to Texas

Eddy made one final effort to gather further evidence against Chambliss. For this purpose, he used information given to him by Mary Frances Cunningham, a sister-in-law of Chambliss (no relation to John Cunningham, the witness who had seen

Former Klansman Bobby Frank Cherry maintains his innocence in the church bombing during a 1997 press conference.

two white men near the church immediately after the blast). According to Mary Frances Cunningham (known by the alias Dale or Gail Tarrant in some accounts of the case), Chambliss once told her that he had seen Bobby Frank Cherry walking with a bomb near the Sixteenth Street Baptist Church the night before the explosion. Eddy was not positive that Cunningham was a trustworthy witness. Still, he realized that he might be able to use Cunningham's words to encourage Cherry to give evidence against Chambliss.

By this time, Cherry had moved away from Birmingham. Eddy flew to Cherry's new home in Texas and arranged for a meeting. He wasted no time in getting to the point of the visit. "Chambliss," he informed Cherry, "said he saw you walking down the alley [by the church] with the bomb." The statement evidently struck a nerve. "Cherry turned white as a sheet,"[55] Eddy reported years later. Though Cherry emphatically denied any knowledge of the bombing, Eddy knew he had shaken the suspect's confidence.

The whole conversation, of course, was a ruse. Eddy had only Mary Frances Cunningham's word that Chambliss had spoken of Cherry at all. Certainly, Chambliss had never told

Baxley's investigative team that he had seen Cherry with the bomb. Still, Eddy thought, Cherry might assume that Chambliss had spoken directly to authorities. If so, Chambliss was betraying Cherry—and violating the Klan code of silence. Under these circumstances, Eddy reasoned, Cherry might be willing, even eager, to testify against Chambliss.

Eddy's plan very nearly worked. At the end of their meeting, a troubled Cherry agreed to consider talking to Eddy in more detail at some future date. But later that night, Cherry made several phone calls to friends in the Birmingham area. These men assured him that Chambliss had never given useful evidence to Eddy and his team and certainly had not implicated Cherry in the bombing in any way. "You lied to me,"[56] Cherry complained when he next spoke with Eddy, and he refused to cooperate any further with the investigation.

Arrest and Trial

Even without Cherry's participation, Baxley and his staffers formally placed Chambliss under arrest on September 24. For the moment, Chambliss was charged only with the murder of one of the girls, Denise McNair. That decision was not made out of disrespect for the other three murdered girls; instead, it was done for practical reasons. According to the law, a person can be tried just once for a given crime. If Chambliss had been charged with all four murders and found not guilty on all counts, he could never have been brought to trial again. By charging him with just one murder, Baxley left open the possibility of charging Chambliss with the other three crimes if he was acquitted and new evidence appeared later on.

The trial began on November 14, 1977. First, Baxley and his team presented testimony from people in the church the day of the explosion. Jurors—nine whites and three blacks—heard from John Cross, the church's pastor in 1963, and from Sarah Collins, the only survivor among the five girls in the restroom that morning. Slowly, prosecutors led the jury through the events of the day. The county coroner

Mary Frances Cunningham

One of the most complex aspects of the bombing case was the testimony of Robert Chambliss's sister-in-law Mary Frances Cunningham. In late 1964, after more than a year of saying very little to federal agents, Cunningham made a series of remarkable claims. First, she reported that Chambliss had told her of watching Cherry running down the street with a bomb the night of September 14-15. During a later interview, she asserted that she had been at the church that night herself and that she had seen Cherry, Chambliss, and Thomas Blanton there. Moreover, Cunningham insisted, she had made that trip to the church with Elizabeth Cobbs (who was not only Chambliss's niece but a niece of Cunningham's as well). Cobbs first confirmed her aunt's statement—then flatly denied it, only adding to the confusion.

Cunningham had yet another story that further complicated the case. Very early on the morning of September 15, 1963, she said, she contacted local sheriff's deputy James Hancock and told him what she had seen. But Hancock refused to take her tip seriously. By the time he arrived at the church, she reported, the bomb had already gone off. When questioned, Hancock cited a slew of recent false alarms to explain why he had been slow to follow up on Cunningham's report. He also claimed that there had been a "personal thing"—presumably an affair—between himself and Cunningham. FBI officials, however, saw Hancock's inaction as further evidence of ties between the Klan and local law enforcement agencies.

Many years later, Cunningham insisted that she had never told the FBI that she had been at the church. The validity of Cunningham's claims will probably never be known. Even without her testimony in 1977, however, Baxley was able to prosecute the case.

Quoted in Frank Sikora, *Until Justice Rolls Down.* Tuscaloosa: University of Alabama Press, 1991, p. 105.

testified to the wounds Denise McNair had suffered. Chris McNair, Denise's father, told the jury that he had said good-bye to his daughter that morning and never seen her alive again. This testimony was designed to establish the severity of the blast and to sway the sympathies of the jurors against the defendant.

After these witnesses, Cobbs gave her testimony. She told the jurors about Chambliss's claim that he had "enough stuff . . . to flatten half of Birmingham,"[57] and she described his statement that the bomb had gone off at the wrong time. On many occasions, she added, she had heard Chambliss say that he would do "anything possible"[58] to stop integration. Defense attorneys tried to cast doubt on Cobbs's testimony. They pointed out that Chambliss's ideas about race were shared by many whites in Birmingham in the early 1960s. They also suggested that after fourteen years, Cobbs might not be recalling Chambliss's words accurately. Still, Cobbs insisted that she had heard exactly what she described.

Cobbs was followed by a few more prosecution witnesses. A woman who had been dating a Klansman in 1963 testified that she had seen an enormous cache of dynamite in Chambliss's home just two weeks before the bombing. Several fire marshals and police investigators told the jury that dynamite had probably been the cause of the explosion and described the discovery and significance of the fishing bobber. Kirthus Glenn testified as well, though defense attorneys challenged her identification of both Chambliss and the car she had seen parked outside the church that night.

The prosecution's witness list, however, was missing two important names. One was Chambliss's sister-in-law Mary Frances Cunningham. Though Cunningham had given investigators potentially valuable information about Chambliss's comments and activities over the years, she flatly refused to testify

By the Numbers

2

Hours the Blanton jury took to agree on a guilty verdict

in open court, and no amount of pleading by Baxley would change her mind. The other missing witness was James Edward Lay, who had reported seeing two white men lurking near the Sixteenth Street Baptist Church two weeks before the bombing. For reasons that are unclear today, Lay had also refused to testify. Baxley and Eddy could only hope that their case was solid even without the testimony of these two witnesses.

The Verdict

Next, it was the turn of the defense to establish the case for Chambliss. Though Chambliss, against the advice of his lawyers, opted not to testify on his own behalf, several friends and family members spoke of his good reputation and fine character. For the most part, however, the defense was content to point out the weaknesses of the prosecution's case. No one, Chambliss's attorneys pointed out, had given evidence that directly implicated their client. They also cautioned jurors not to let raw emotion get in the way of the verdict. The issue before the jury, the lawyers argued, was simply whether Chambliss was guilty or innocent. Jurors were not in court to right a terrible wrong or to avenge the bombing; they were there only to weigh the evidence.

As the defense had predicted, prosecutors played directly to the jurors' emotions in their final summary. "Today," Baxley told the jury, "is Denise McNair's birthday. And if she had lived, she would have been twenty-six." He displayed pictures of the corpses of the four girls and talked about the enormity of the crime. Then he reviewed the testimony of Glenn, Cobbs, and the other witnesses and briefly reviewed the case against Chambliss. "The crime was against all of us," he concluded, "against the people of Birmingham and the state of Alabama. Give Denise McNair a birthday present."[59]

The jury did exactly that. After spending parts of two days in deliberations, the jurors unanimously found Chambliss guilty of the death of Denise McNair. He was sentenced to life in prison. One man behind the bombing had been caught. The death of Denise McNair had been avenged.

Two More Trials

Bill Baxley was delighted with the successful prosecution of Robert Chambliss in the church bombing case. He hoped, too, that Chambliss's conviction would soon lead to charges against Cash, Cherry, Blanton, and possibly others. It was possible, he believed, that Chambliss would implicate his former friends now that he was safely behind bars. But Chambliss did not. Instead, he strenuously maintained his innocence. As he wrote in a 1978 letter begging Baxley for clemency, "I have never Bombed any thing[,] never killed any Body and never be[e]n in Tommy Blanton's car in my life."[60] Chambliss died in 1985 without admitting his role in the blast or implicating anyone else.

Though he could not obtain Chambliss's cooperation, Baxley had a second plan. He hoped that the conviction of Chambliss would alarm others who had participated in the plot. If so, Baxley planned to offer other suspects a deal: If they would admit their guilt in the bombing and testify against their fellow conspirators, he would give them a lighter prison sentence than Chambliss had received. Immediately after the verdict in the Chambliss case was announced, in fact, Baxley sent Bob Eddy to offer Thomas Blanton precisely this agreement.

But if Blanton was frightened by the guilty verdict against Chambliss, he showed no sign of it. Instead, he turned down the offer and continued to insist that he knew nothing about the case. Investigators offered Bobby Frank Cherry a similar deal with no greater success. Cherry's unwillingness to accept the terms was a particular blow to Baxley. Cherry, he said years later, was "mean and vicious and unrepentant, and it was devastating to realize that we were never going to get a chance to bring him to justice."[61]

In 1994 white supremacist Byron de la Beckwith was convicted for the 1963 assassination of civil rights leader Medgar Evers.

Baxley would have continued pushing forward on the case. In 1978, however, he decided not to run for reelection as attorney general, instead mounting an ultimately unsuccessful campaign for governor. His replacement as the state's chief prosecutor showed no interest in pursuing the case against Cherry, Blanton, Cash, or any of the other suspects. Baxley had succeeded in putting Chambliss behind bars. Now, however, the case seemed to have come to an end once again.

The FBI Returns

The bombing of the Sixteenth Street Baptist Church was just one of several civil rights–related murder cases in the South during the early 1960s. Like the church bombing, most of these cases were not solved right away. Often, federal officials had strong evidence indicating the guilt of one or more people in the crimes. But as in Birmingham, the culture in these other parts of the South at the time made it difficult to convict white defendants of killing blacks—or even of killing white civil rights activists. Some suspects stood trial on less serious charges, such as conspiring to deprive others of their civil rights, and a few did spend time in prison after juries found them guilty. Most, though, escaped any punishment at all.

Bill Baxley's successful action against Robert Chambliss during the late 1970s, however, had showed prosecutors that times were changing. In the wake of the Chambliss verdict, federal and state governments began reopening old civil rights cases and bringing charges against suspects. In 1994, for example, white supremacist Byron de la Beckwith was convicted of the murder of civil rights leader Medgar Evers thirty-one years earlier; in 1998, Klan leader Sam Bowers was convicted of 1966 killing of Mississippi activist Vernon Dahmer.

In 1995, FBI officials, following the lead of these prosecutors, reopened the church bombing case. The decision came as a surprise to Ben Herren, one of two detectives assigned to lead the investigation. As a Birmingham native, Herren knew very well that law enforcement officials had been able to prosecute

Steps in a Trial

A criminal trial follows certain predetermined steps, as follows:

1 **Prosecutors file charges** against one or more suspects in a case.

2 **The case is assigned** to a particular judge.

3 **Lawyers for the prosecution** and the defense work with the judge to choose a jury from among the citizens of the community where the trial will take place.

4 **Lawyers for both sides** make opening statements, outlining the case for and against the defendant.

5 **The prosecution calls witnesses** to testify against the defendant. The defense may question, or cross-examine, these witnesses.

6 **The defense calls witnesses** of its own, whom the prosecution may also cross-examine.

7 **Lawyers for both sides** give final closing statements.

8 **The jurors deliberate,** or consider the strength of the case, and arrive at a verdict.

9 **If the jury finds** the defendant guilty, the judge—or in some jurisdictions, the jury—determines a sentence.

only one of the five original suspects. In his opinion, nothing had changed. "This is a 30-year-old case," he told his supervisor, FBI agent Rob Langford. "There's nothing new, no dying confession." But Langford still insisted on undertaking the investigation. "The people of Alabama need this looked at,"[62] he told Herren.

Herren's concerns were legitimate. Decades had passed since the killings at the Sixteenth Street Baptist Church. Those witnesses to the crime who had been young adults in 1963 were now past middle age. Those in their forties or beyond were elderly or dead. Early in the investigation, Herren and his partner, William Fleming, made a list of the people interviewed by FBI agents during the 1960s in connection with the case. About 130 of these people, they discovered, were no longer alive. Under these circumstances, Herren and Fleming knew, further research into the bombing case would be very difficult.

The remaining suspects were growing old, too—and fewer. Herman Cash had died in 1994, the year before Langford reopened the case. Thomas Blanton, a young hothead in 1963, was now approaching sixty. The only other surviving suspect, Bobby Frank Cherry, was almost ten years older. The odds were good that neither man would live many years longer. The advancing ages of Blanton and Cherry forced FBI officials to act quickly to reopen the case—or choose to close it forever.

Research and Interviews

Like Baxley and his team nearly twenty years earlier, Herren and Fleming began by examining every record of the case they could find. Between 1995 and 1997 they and their staff read the transcript of Chambliss's trial, scrutinized 1960s interviews with Blanton and Cherry, and studied the notes of virtually every state and federal agent who had worked on the case. Unlike Baxley and his staff, who had been granted access only to a limited number of materials, Herren and Fleming were able to examine any of the estimated ten thousand documents about the case that the FBI had collected over the years.

Herren and Fleming also listened to the FBI's cache of secret tape recordings made by agents during the 1960s, tapes that Baxley and his investigators had not known existed. Most of the recordings were old and scratchy. Even with electronic enhancement, it was often difficult to make out individual words or to determine who was speaking at any given time. Still, the investigators knew that the tapes could be extremely valuable in pointing a way toward a solution of the case.

Once the research stage of the investigation was complete, Herren and Fleming began the task of questioning witnesses. Until this point, the reopening of the case had been kept a secret; now, with the investigation moving into the public eye, FBI officials formally announced that the bombing case was again being pursued. "We don't want to raise expectations too high," said a spokesman for the agency. "[But] we would not have reopened the case if we did not believe there was a basis for it, and a possibility of solving it."[63]

From 1997 to 2000, both Herren and Fleming spent much of their time

William Fleming was one of two detectives who conducted a five-year investigation into the church bombing that concluded in 2000.

in interviews. The job was grueling and often maddening. The two men visited former and current Klansmen at their homes all around the country. Most of these Klansmen were old, most were still passionately segregationist, and most gave the investigators no information whatever. "Nobody was telling us anything," Fleming recalled. "It was very, very tiresome, like beating your head against a stone wall."[64] Nonetheless, little by little, the two men and their team of investigators made progress.

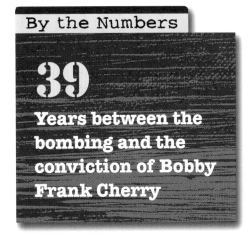

By the Numbers

39

Years between the bombing and the conviction of Bobby Frank Cherry

Cherry's Press Conference

The team's greatest breakthrough, in fact, came early on. In 1997, Herren and Fleming paid an unexpected visit to Bobby Frank Cherry's home in Texas, where they and Cherry talked for more than four hours. During this discussion, Cherry boasted of taking part in several violent acts during the civil rights years. On the subject of the church bombing, however, the sixty-seven-year-old Cherry was less forthcoming. He flatly denied participation and repeated, as he had years earlier, that he had no idea who had carried out the plot.

Still, even though Cherry had not given them the answers they wanted, the investigators were heartened by the interview. Cherry, they realized, was tense and angry, and that anger might soon drive him to make statements he would regret. The day after Cherry's talk with the FBI agents, in fact, Cherry held a press conference to accuse the bureau of harassment. He gave an angry, rambling speech accusing federal agents of making him the target of a "witch hunt."[65] Cherry's charges against the FBI were serious, and the reopened bombing investigation had become news, so journalists quickly spread the details of the press conference throughout the country.

That publicity was Cherry's undoing. Among the people who heard about the press conference was a Montana woman named Willadean Brogdon. Brogdon immediately recognized Cherry's name, and for good reason: In 1970, she had become the third of his five wives. The marriage, however, had been miserable, and the couple divorced after three years. Brogdon had lost touch with Cherry, so his press conference took her by surprise. More than that, however, it infuriated her. Cherry's statements so enraged Brogdon, in fact, that she drove 250 miles to the nearest FBI office and demanded to see an agent on the spot. Her story, she informed the agent, would help the bureau put her former husband in jail. During their three years of marriage, she explained, Cherry had often boasted to her about his participation in the bombing. "He didn't put the bomb together,"[66] she clarified. But according to her account, Cherry had cheerfully admitted lighting the fuse.

More Witnesses

Willadean Brogdon was not the only witness to come forward after hearing about Cherry's press conference. Alabama resident Michael Goings also contacted federal officials when he learned that Cherry was under investigation for the bombing. Several years earlier, he informed FBI agents, he had heard Cherry brag about blowing up a church. Like Brogdon, Goings went to great personal trouble to tell his story. Seriously ill with lung disease, Goings had enormous difficulty speaking. Still, he considered his information too vital not to make the effort.

Nor was Brogdon even the only one of Cherry's relatives to offer testimony against him. Cherry's granddaughter Teresa Stacy, now grown, told agents that Cherry had told her stories about the bombing several times when she was younger. "He said he helped blow up a bunch of niggers back in Birmingham," Stacy reported. "He seemed rather jovial." Like Goings and Brogdon, Stacy had reacted quickly upon learning of Cherry's press conference. "I knew he was lying," she explained. "I called the news people. They put me on hold for a long time. I hung up the phone and called the FBI."[67] Before long, Stacy too had become a witness for the prosecution.

Finding Willadean

The agents who investigated the reopened bombing case during the 1990s were not completely shocked to see Willadean Brogdon come forward. They had heard from various sources that Bobby Frank Cherry had once been married to a red-haired woman named Willadean, and they knew that the couple had exchanged bitter words throughout their marriage. Investigators believed that this woman might have inside knowledge that would help them convict Cherry, along with enough resentment left over from their brief marriage to be willing to tell what she knew. But Brogdon had long since left Alabama, and no one in or around Birmingham seemed to know where she was. Nor had any of Cherry's seven children kept in touch with their onetime stepmother. With higher priorities in the case, agents spent only limited time looking for Cherry's former wife. They were delighted when Brogdon, now gray-haired and living in Montana, came to them—and more delighted still when they heard what she had to say about her former husband.

Giving the press conference was a serious mistake on Cherry's part. But he soon compounded that blunder with another. In a statement addressed to journalists and investigators alike, Cherry said that he could not have planted a bomb on the night of September 14. He had spent the entire evening at home watching wrestling on television, he said, and caring for his wife, who according to Cherry had been sick for quite some time with cancer. But after researching Birmingham television schedules in 1963, Mississippi reporter Jerry Mitchell determined that no wrestling matches had been broadcast that evening. And though Cherry's wife did die of cancer, her illness was not diagnosed until well after the bombing. Agents quickly concluded that Cherry's alibi was faked.

Tape Recordings

Thomas Blanton, the other surviving suspect, held no press conferences and had no surprise witnesses speak out against him. But as far as Herren and Fleming were concerned, the evidence against Blanton was already strong. The night before the bombing, Kirthus Glenn had seen Blanton's car parked outside the church; the morning of the explosion, other witnesses had seen it again. And though Blanton had claimed to have been with his girlfriend, Jean Casey, for most of the evening, investigators noticed that the details of what he and Casey did—and when—changed each time he talked to agents. "He remembers everything about that day [September 14],"

Prosecutor Doug Jones arrives at the Birmingham courthouse for Bobby Frank Cherry's trial in 2002.

noted one member of the investigative team. "But when it comes to that night, he gets fuzzy."[68]

Even more incriminating were the tapes that the FBI had made of Blanton's conversations during the 1960s. FBI officials believed that all these tapes, not merely the ones obtained in Mitchell Burns's car, would now be admissible in a trial. They planned to argue that the recordings had been made in part to prevent further violence; thus, the bugs were necessary to protect national security. During the 1990s, they argued, judges often authorized wiretaps and hidden microphones for exactly this purpose. Under these circumstances, investigators believed, it made sense to treat the 1960s recordings as if they had been made at the time the case had been reopened—and to enter them into the trial record as evidence.

Certainly, the recordings were damning. "I like to go shooting, I like to go fishing, I like to go bombing,"[69] Blanton bragged to Burns in one of the tapes. On another occasion, Blanton could be heard to remark, "They ain't going to catch me when I bomb my next church."[70] On a third, Blanton explained that he and some friends had spent an evening shortly before September 15, 1963, "at a meeting where we planned the bomb."[71] It was difficult to mistake the meaning of any of these statements.

Blanton's Trial

In 2000, federal agents issued murder charges against Blanton and Cherry, and the two men were placed under arrest. U.S. attorney Doug Jones was assigned to lead the prosecution against the two men. Immediately, however, Cherry's lawyer petitioned to have the charges against his client dropped altogether. Cherry, he claimed, was suffering from dementia. He would not be able to understand the proceedings or help prepare his own defense. When a mental health evaluation seemed to bear out the lawyer's contention, Judge James Garrett ruled that Cherry should not stand trial.

This decision was a serious blow for the prosecution and for the friends and families of the four victims of the bombing, who had by now waited nearly forty years for justice. Jones and his staff quickly protested the ruling, claiming that Cherry was faking mental incompetence. Although Garrett did not reverse his original decision, he did agree to order more psychiatric evaluations for Cherry. For the moment, though, the prosecutors' original plan—to try the two suspects together—would no longer be possible.

The trial of Thomas Blanton began in April 2001, even as the reevaluations of Cherry's mental health were continuing. The prosecution introduced the tapes as evidence against Blanton, playing several excerpts for Garrett and the eight

Timeline of the Birmingham Church Bombings

September 15:
The bombing of the Sixteenth Street Baptist Church kills Cynthia Wesley, Denise McNair, Addie Mae Collins, and Carole Robertson.

September 24:
Robert Chambliss is arrested and charged with the murder of Denise McNair.

Baxley forms a task force to investigate the case.

November 14:
Chambliss's trial begins. Jurors later find Chambliss guilty, and he is sentenced to life in prison.

Five suspects' names are sent to J. Edgar Hoover, who declines to prosecute.

September 30:
Robert Chambliss, Charles Cagle, and John Wesley Hall are arrested on charges of possession of dynamite.

The federal government allows Baxley's task force to examine FBI files.

Alabama attorney general Bill Baxley reopens the case.

whites and four blacks who made up the jury. Unfortunately for the prosecution, Kirthus Glenn, Elizabeth Cobbs, and several other earlier witnesses had died since Bill Baxley had tried Robert Chambliss. But prosecutors brought in two FBI agents who had investigated the case during the 1960s, and they testified about their suspicions of Blanton at that time. The prosecution also brought up the inconsistencies in Blanton's alibi for the night before the bombing.

Blanton's defense attorneys used a variety of arguments on behalf of their client. They pointed out that no physical evidence connected Blanton with the crime. As with Robert

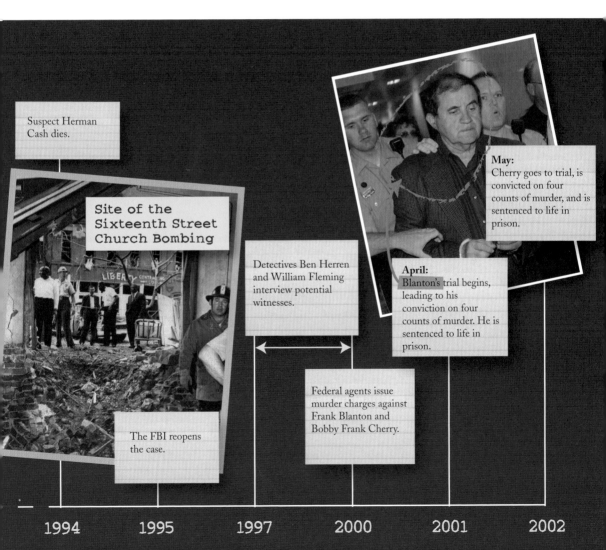

Suspect Herman Cash dies.

Site of the Sixteenth Street Church Bombing

May: Cherry goes to trial, is convicted on four counts of murder, and is sentenced to life in prison.

Detectives Ben Herren and William Fleming interview potential witnesses.

April: Blanton's trial begins, leading to his conviction on four counts of murder. He is sentenced to life in prison.

The FBI reopens the case.

Federal agents issue murder charges against Frank Blanton and Bobby Frank Cherry.

1994   1995   1997   2000   2001   2002

A handcuffed Thomas Blanton Jr. is escorted from the courthouse after a jury convicted him of murder for his role in the bombing.

Chambliss, no witness claimed to have seen Blanton making, carrying, or placing the bomb. The attorneys attacked the evidence on the tapes, too. Blanton's conversations sounded incriminating, they admitted, but in reality Blanton and his friends were harmless; they were just "rednecks driving around, drinking, running their mouths,"[72] claimed one lawyer.

Blanton's lawyers also vehemently challenged the prosecution's use of the tapes. Because the recordings had not been admissible as evidence when originally made, defense lawyers noted, they should have remained unacceptable in court. Moreover, Blanton's attorneys claimed, prosecutors should have played entire tape recordings of the discussions rather than excerpts. "This is a four-minute segment of a lengthy conversation," said defense attorney John Robbins of one such excerpt. "[I] don't think you can put that four minutes in its proper context without the other 26 minutes."[73]

The jurors, however, were not swayed by these arguments. After only brief deliberations, they found Blanton guilty on four counts of murder—one for each of the four girls killed in the bombing. Blanton, then sixty-two, was sentenced to life in prison. African Americans throughout Birmingham cheered the verdict. And in a twist that black residents of Birmingham in 1963 could scarcely have imagined, so did many whites. Two men had now been brought to justice in the church bombing case—and prosecutors still hoped to add Bobby Frank Cherry to that list.

Cherry's Trial

They soon got their chance. Several months after Blanton was found guilty, a team of psychologists assigned to test Cherry's mental health determined that he had been faking dementia and was fit to stand trial. After reviewing the psychologists' reports, Garrett ordered Cherry's trial to proceed. In May 2002, a year after Blanton had been found guilty, the trial of the last surviving suspect in the church bombing case began.

As had been true of Blanton's trial, several witnesses in the case had died or were too sick to testify. But others—including Willadean Brogdon, Cherry's ex-wife, and Teresa Stacy, his granddaughter—testified that Cherry had often spoken of his involvement in the bombing. Prosecutor Doug Jones also pointed out that Cherry's alibi for the evening of September 14, 1963, had been proven wrong. And while most of the FBI's tapes from the 1960s did not include Cherry's words, a few did seem to implicate him in the plot, and prosecutors played those excerpts for the jury.

But Cherry's defense attorneys proclaimed his innocence. His lawyers painted Brogdon as a vengeful ex-wife willing to lie in order to get her former husband in trouble, and they

Bobby Frank Cherry was convicted of four counts of murder in 2002. His conviction finally brought the bombing case to a close.

pointed out that Stacy had a history of substance abuse. They also produced two of Cherry's grandsons, who swore that their grandfather had never discussed the church bombing with them. The FBI, lawyers complained, had decided that Cherry was guilty and then had manufactured evidence to make that seem to be the case. Cherry's defenders implored the nine whites and three blacks on the jury to consider the evidence carefully and not to assume their client's guilt.

The jurors took their time over the verdict. They deliberated for a number of hours before returning to the courtroom and unanimously agreeing that Cherry, like Blanton, was guilty of four counts of murder. After thirty-nine years, the church bombing case had at last come to an end. Of the original five suspects, two—Herman Cash and Troy Ingram—had died before they could be put on trial, but Chambliss, Blanton, and now Cherry had been brought to justice. "I feel at ease now," said Sarah Collins Rudolph, the sister of Addie Mae and the only one of the five girls to survive the blast in 1963. "We have been waiting on this day for a long time."[74]

Justice Delayed

In one sense, the guilty verdicts in the church bombing case came entirely too late. Only days after the blast that ripped through the Sixteenth Street Baptist Church and killed four young girls, FBI agents already had a clear sense of who was responsible; two years later, after a massive investigation into the crime, they had no doubts. Yet it took decades for officials to bring charges against the bombers. As a result of this inaction, Robert Chambliss lived for fourteen undeserving years as a free man after the explosion, Thomas Blanton and Bobby Frank Cherry nearly forty. Justice would have been better served by bringing all three men—and probably Troy Ingram and Herman Cash—to trial years earlier.

But given the racism that pervaded Alabama at the time of the bombing, the sad reality is that justice probably would not have been served by a trial in the mid-1960s. In all likelihood, a jury of Alabama residents at the time would have acquitted the defendants on charges of murder and perhaps on lesser charges as well. As historian Diane McWhorter and others have demonstrated, too many state and city officials during the 1960s were tied to organizations such as the Ku Klux Klan. Too many ordinary white citizens were prepared to maintain segregation no matter the cost. Birmingham in 1963 was simply not a place that was responsive to the suffering of blacks.

That is not to suggest that the conduct of FBI officials was above reproach. J. Edgar Hoover's distaste for the civil rights movement has made many observers question his commitment to finding the bombers. Likewise, observers throughout the years have been troubled by the bureau's covert connections with Gary Thomas Rowe and other informers. Even if FBI

Today, the renovated Sixteenth Street Baptist Church stands as a moving memorial to the four little girls who lost their lives in the 1963 bombing.

officials had strong reasons not to make arrests—notably an awareness of the political realities of 1960s Alabama and a recognition that much of the FBI's best evidence could not be used in court—it is possible that Hoover's hostility toward civil rights and his desire to protect informers clouded his judgment and encouraged him to drop a case that he might otherwise have won.

Similar questions have arisen about why FBI officials never told Bill Baxley about the bureau's surveillance tapes during the 1970s. The FBI asserts that this was a simple oversight, but Baxley has always wondered if the FBI's leaders were deliberately trying to conceal evidence. If he had been able to use the tapes in 1977, Baxley insists, he could have convicted not just Chambliss, but Blanton and Cherry as well. By not giving the tapes to him, Baxley once complained, "the FBI handed Tom Blanton a get-out-of-jail-free card good for 24 years."[75]

"Justice Will Come"

Nor have the verdicts changed much in the lives of Birmingham's African Americans. Racism is still present in Birmingham. Blacks in Alabama, as in other states, are disproportionately poor and undereducated; they have lower life expectancies and higher rates of unemployment than whites. The convictions of Chambliss, Blanton, and Cherry did not erase the racism that underlay the original crime—or the shameful responses of many white Alabamians to it. The guilty verdicts could not place Birmingham's black community on an equal footing with the city's white population. All they could do was to put the surviving bombers in prison.

Still, in one sense that was enough. Though thirty-nine years was too long for the friends and families of the victims to wait for justice, waiting thirty-nine years was far better than never having justice at all. The bombing was a terrible crime, but the crime was made far worse because authorities were unable—or unwilling—to bring the criminals to trial. The explosion was the work of a small group of angry, frustrated, violent men; the inability to pursue the case, on the other hand, was the work of an entire society.

In this way, the guilty verdicts represented the righting of not one tragic wrong, but two. In 1963, the criminal justice system maintained one set of standards and rules for blacks and another set for whites. Now, jurors of both races had sifted through the evidence against Chambliss, Blanton, and Cherry and determined that the men were guilty—even though the killers were white and their victims black. By convicting the three men, the jurors not only avenged the tragedy of that Sunday morning, they also declared that the era of racism and injustice, in Birmingham and elsewhere, was finally over.

Indeed, though observers mourned the years that had been lost, most took the opportunity to cheer the jurors' decisions and to look with renewed hope to the future. Three men had gone to prison; the case had finally been closed. Though the convictions would not bring the dead girls back, the families and friends of Addie Mae Collins, Carole Robertson, Cynthia Wesley, and Denise McNair knew that something important had been accomplished. "The price of freedom is suffering, perseverance, and endurance," said civil rights veteran Fred Shuttlesworth upon learning that Bobby Frank Cherry had at last been convicted. "It is ridiculous that justice can be delayed, but America has said today that justice will come even if it takes 40 years."[76]

Notes

Introduction: A Troubled City

1. Quoted in Diane McWhorter, *Carry Me Home*. New York: Simon and Schuster, 2001, p. 21.

2. Quoted in Henry Hampton and Steve Fayer, *Voices of Freedom*. New York: Bantam, 1990, p. 123.

3. Quoted in Hampton and Fayer, *Voices of Freedom*, p. 134.

4. Paul Hemphill, *Leaving Birmingham*. New York: Viking, 1993, opposite page 226.

Chapter One: The Crime

5. Quoted in Frank Sikora, *Until Justice Rolls Down*. Tuscaloosa: University of Alabama Press, 1991, p. 10.

6. Elizabeth H. Cobbs/Petric J. Smith, *Long Time Coming*. Birmingham, AL: Crane Hill, 1994, p. 94.

7. Quoted in Sikora, *Until Justice Rolls Down*, p. 11.

8. Quoted in McWhorter, *Carry Me Home*, p. 525.

9. Quoted in Hampton and Fayer, *Voices of Freedom*, p. 173.

10. Quoted in *Time*, "The Sunday School Bombing," September 27, 1963, no page available.

11. Quoted in Hampton and Fayer, *Voices of Freedom*, p. 176.

12. Quoted in Hemphill, *Leaving Birmingham*, p. 155.

13. Quoted in Sikora, *Until Justice Rolls Down*, p. 21.

14. McWhorter, *Carry Me Home*, p. 259.

15. Cobbs/Smith, *Long Time Coming*, p. 52.

16. Quoted in Gary May, *The Informant*. New Haven, CT: Yale University Press, 2005, p. 14.

17. Quoted in Pamela Colloff, "The Sins of the Father," *Texas Monthly*, April 2000, no page available.

18. Quoted in McWhorter, *Carry Me Home*, p. 530.

19. Quoted in Hemphill, *Leaving Birmingham*, p. 155.

Chapter Two: The Investigation Begins

20. Quoted in May, *Informant*, p. 89.

21. Quoted in McWhorter, *Carry Me Home*, p. 524.

22. Quoted in Sikora, *Until Justice Rolls Down*, p. 98.

23. Quoted in McWhorter, *Carry Me Home*, p. 516.

24. Quoted in May, *Informant*, p. 79.

Chapter Three: The Investigation Stalls

25. Quoted in Colloff, "Sins of the Father," no page available.

26. Quoted in Sikora, *Until Justice Rolls Down*, p. 79.

27. Quoted in May, *Informant*, p. 97.

28. Quoted in Sikora, *Until Justice Rolls Down*, p. 73.

29. Quoted in Colloff, "Sins of the Father," no page available.

30. Quoted in May, *Informant*, p. 96.

31. Quoted in May, *Informant*, p. 90.

32. Quoted in May, *Informant*, p. 91.

33. May, *Informant*, p. 98.

34. Quoted in *Time*, "Farce in Birmingham," October 18, 1963, no page available.

35. Quoted in McWhorter, *Carry Me Home*, p. 149.

36. Quoted in May, *Informant*, p. 97.

37. Quoted in Sikora, *Until Justice Rolls Down*, p. 71.

38. Quoted in Rick Bragg, "Man Says Dead Girls' Photo Led Him to Become Informer," *New York Times*, May 16, 2002.

39. Quoted in Sikora, *Until Justice Rolls Down*, p. 94.

40. Quoted in Cobbs/Smith, *Long Time Coming*, p, 89.

41. Quoted in Cobbs/Smith, *Long Time Coming*, p. 98.

42. Quoted in May, *Informant*, p. 97.

43. Quoted in Colloff, "Sins of the Father," no page available.

44. Quoted in May, *Informant*, p. 103.

Chapter Four: Reopening the Case

45. Quoted in Margaret Kimberley, "Condoleezza Rice and the Birmingham Bombing Victims," www.blackcommentator.com/52/52_rice.html.

46. Quoted in Sikora, *Until Justice Rolls Down*, pp. 39–40.

47. Quoted in Sikora, *Until Justice Rolls Down*, p. 41.

48. Quoted in Sikora, *Until Justice Rolls Down*, p. 51.

49. Cobbs/Smith, *Long Time Coming*, p. 154.

50. Cobbs/Smith, *Long Time Coming*, p. 155.

51. Cobbs/Smith, *Long Time Coming*, p. 144.

52. Quoted in Sikora, *Until Justice Rolls Down*, p. 96.

53. Cobbs/Smith, *Long Time Coming*, p. 154.

54. Cobbs/Smith, *Long Time Coming*, p. 155.

55. Quoted in Colloff, "Sins of the Father," no page available.

56. Quoted in Sikora, *Until Justice Rolls Down*, p. 109.

57. Quoted in Cobbs/Smith, *Long Time Coming*, p. 89.

58. Quoted in Sikora, *Until Justice Rolls Down*, p. 141.

59. Quoted in Sikora, *Until Justice Rolls Down*, p. 153.

Chapter Five: Two More Trials

60. Quoted in Cobbs/Smith, *Long Time Coming*, p. 222.

61. Quoted in Colloff, "Sins of the Father," no page available.

62. Quoted in Bill Lambrecht, "'Unsung Heroes,'" *St. Louis Post-Dispatch*, November 24, 2002.

63. Quoted in Adam Cohen, "Back to 'Bombingham,'" *Time*, July 21, 1997, no page available.

64. Quoted in Lambrecht, "'Unsung Heroes.'"

65. Quoted in Colloff, "Sins of the Father," no page available.

66. Quoted in Christopher John Farley, "The Ghosts of Alabama," *Time*, May 29, 2000, no page available.

67. Quoted in Rick Bragg, "Survivor of '63 Bomb Recalls Glass Shards and a Sister Lost," *New York Times*, May 18, 2002.

68. Quoted in Frank Sikora, "Tales from the Tapes Help Convict Birmingham Bomber," *Time*, May 2, 2001, no page available.

69. Quoted in CNN, "Birmingham Church Bomber Guilty, Gets Four Life Terms," May 1, 2001. www.africanamericans.com/BirminghamBombing.htm.

70. Quoted in Sikora, "Tales from the Tapes," no page available.

71. Quoted in CNN.com, "One Guilty Verdict, One Possible Trial to Come in 1963 Alabama Church Bombing." http://transcripts.cnn.com/TRANSCRIPTS/0105/02/bp.00.html.

72. Quoted in Crime Library, "Birmingham Church Bombing by the Ku Klux Klan." www.crimelibrary.com/terrorists_spies/terrorists/birmingham_church/11.html.

73. Quoted in CNN.com, "One Guilty Verdict."

74. Quoted in Crime Library, "Birmingham Church Bombings."

Afterword: Justice Delayed

75. Quoted in Kevin Sack, "FBI Denies an Effort to Hinder Alabama's Bombing Inquiry," *New York Times*, May 4, 2001.

76. Quoted in Dahleen Glanton, "Klansman Convicted in Bombing," *Chicago Tribune*, May 23, 2002.

For Further Reading

Books

Sara Bullard, *Free At Last: A History of the Civil Rights Movement and Those Who Died in the Struggle.* New York: Oxford University Press, 1994. A basic history of the civil rights movement.

Elizabeth H. Cobbs/Petric J. Smith, *Long Time Coming.* Birmingham, AL: Crane Hill, 1994. An account of the bombing case by the niece of Robert Chambliss; culminates in the events of the 1977 investigation and trial.

Fred J. Cook, *The Ku Klux Klan: America's Recurring Nightmare.* New York: Julian Messner, 1989. A description of the Ku Klux Klan and its activities through the years, with particular emphasis on the 1960s.

Henry Hampton and Steve Fayer, *Voices of Freedom.* New York: Bantam, 1990. Descriptions of the civil rights movement by people who were actively involved in it as well as observers. Includes a section on the Birmingham church bombing.

Regine I. Heberlein, ed., *White Supremacists.* San Diego: Greenhaven, 2002. Describes the Ku Klux Klan and other white supremacist groups, focusing on the activities of these groups both today and in the past.

Paul Hemphill, *Leaving Birmingham.* New York: Viking, 1993. A memoir by a white man who grew up in Birmingham and was a young adult during the civil rights era.

Sheela Ramaprian, *The FBI.* Children's Press, 2003. The structure, the workings, and the mission of the FBI and its role in fighting crime.

Frank Sikora, *Until Justice Rolls Down.* Tuscaloosa: University of Alabama Press, 1991. A straightforward account of the bombing case with particular emphasis on Bill Baxley's reopening of the case and the 1977 trial of Robert Chambliss.

Periodicals

Bill Baxley, "Why Did the FBI Hold Back Evidence?" *New York Times*, May 3, 2001.

Rick Bragg, "Survivor of '63 Bomb Recalls Glass Shards and a Sister Lost," *New York Times*, May 18, 2002.

Pamela Colloff, "The Sins of the Father," *Texas Monthly*, April 2000.

Dahleen Glanton, "Klansman Convicted in Bombing," *Chicago Tribune*, May 23, 2002.

Bill Lambrecht, "'Unsung Heroes,'" *St. Louis Post-Dispatch*, November 24, 2002.

Frank Sikora, "Tales from the Tapes Help Convict Birmingham Bomber," *Time*, May 2, 2001.

Chanda Temple, "Cherry Convicted," *Birmingham News*, May 23, 2002.

Time, "The Sunday School Bombing," September 27, 1963.

Web Site Sources

"Birmingham, Alabama, and the Civil Rights Movement in 1963." www.english.uiuc.edu/maps/poets/m_r/randall/birmingham.htm. An assortment of newspaper and magazine articles, first-person accounts, and other information relating to Birmingham in the early 1960s, much of it focused on the bombing. Includes descriptions of the lives of the four girls killed in the blast.

Crime Library, "Birmingham Church Bombing by the Ku Klux Klan." www.crimelibrary.com/terrorists_spies/terrorists/birmingham_church/index.html. An overview of the bombing case, including investigations, trials, and information on the Ku Klux Klan and the civil rights movement.

PBS Online News Hour, "Pursuing the Past: The Birmingham Church Bombing." www.pbs.org/newshour/media/clarion/kc_birmingham.html. Describes the case and the various investigations, culminating in the conviction of Bobby Frank Cherry in 2002.

Internet Sources

CNN.com, "One Guilty Verdict, One Possible Trial to Come in 1963 Alabama Church Bombing." http://transcripts.cnn.com/TRANSCRIPTS/0105/02/bp.00.html. A roundtable discussion involving prosecutors, defense attorneys, and other commentators held immediately after Thomas Blanton was found guilty.

Index

Picture Credits

Cover, AP/Wide World photo

AP/Wide World Photo, 7, 10, 13, 15, 16, 23, 33, 38, 48, 68, 78, 82, 86, 88

© Bettmann/CORBIS, 9, 21, 24, 27, 30, 36, 44, 52, 59, 63

Tamia Dowlatabadi, 22

© Kevin Fleming/CORBIS, 91

© CORBIS, 26

Time-Life Pictures/Getty Images, 15(top), 18, 41, 61, 74

About the Author

Stephen Currie is the author of more than forty books, including a number of works on history and some historical fiction. Among his books for Lucent are *Life in a Wild West Show*, *The Olympic Games*, and *Adoption*. He is also a teacher. He grew up in Illinois and now lives with his family in upstate New York.